A SOMERSET PARISH
1895–1965

Memories of village life in

High Ham, Low Ham & Henley

Published by
The High Ham Parish Community Project, Somerset, England
www.communityhistory.btck.co.uk
e: hhparishbooks@gmail.com
Copyright ©The High Ham Parish Community Project
Copyright of photographs resides with their owners and/or photographers
Copyright of the quotations resides with their authors

First published 2014

Research by Amanda Chuter, Caroline Dickens, Sara Ellis, Viv Hall and Kate Lynch
Design & layout by Hannah Marchant at The Somerton Printery,
with The High Ham Parish Community Project

All rights reserved. No part of this publication may be reproduced, stored in a retrieved system or transmitted, in any form or by any means, electronic, mechanical, photocopying, recording or otherwise without the prior permission of the publisher

Printed and bound by The Somerton Printery, Somerton, Somerset, England

A catalogue record for this book is available from the British Library

ISBN **978-0-9929953-0-0**

Contents

	Page
Acknowledgements	4
Foreword	5
Map	6
The Turn of the Century	7
The War Years 1914-18	10
Shakespeare at The Court	15
The War Years 1939-45	17
The Low Ham Roman Villa	30
High Days and Holidays	35
Life at School	55
Farming	71
Water and Electricity	90
Trades and other work	93
Provisions, Pub, Policeman and Nurse	96
Transport	104
Footnotes	114
The Photographs and Memories	119
High Ham Parish Community Project	119
The Somerset Heritage Centre	119

Acknowledgements

Those who have lent photographs and whose words are quoted are listed below. However, many more family members, friends, and others who have had a connection with the villages, have taken an interest in the project and given introductions and information. This book would not have been possible without everyone who has helped. This is largely a collection of personal memories, anecdotes and family photographs, rather than a piece of academic research, and if there are omissions or errors then corrections and further information will be very welcome. Special thanks to Graeme Best and Hannah Marchant at the Somerton Printery for their help with the design and printing of the book. Thanks also to Jennifer Heywood for sharing the archive of her father, the late Stanley Lewis, Sue Young for proof-reading, and Somerset County Council Heritage Service for their assistance.

The following individuals and families have contributed the photographs, memories and text:

Gigi and Steve Allen • Sam Astill • Shirley Badman • Doug Bown
Pete Brown • Gwen Chubb • Gillian Clothier • Karen and Owen Cook • Pam Coombes • Peggy Coombes
Len and Margaret Cox • Diana Crossman • Norman Crossman • Molly Cullen • Tony Cullen
Dennis and Dulcie Davis • Isobelle Dennis • Diana Dunthorn • Una Dyer
Ken and Jean Edmunds • David and Paula Fisher • Jack Fisher
Henry Ford • Steve Fouracre • Mary Freeman* • Frank Gibbs • Amanda Hann • Freda Hayes
Sandra Hayes • Jennifer Heywood • Maggie Hibberd • Brian Hill • Brian Howell • Michael Hughes
Les and Jenny Inder • Mike Jenkins • Sheila Jewell • Edith Kiddle*
Les* and Nora Langford • Linda Lavis* • Anna McCallion • Tony Meaker • Mary Ann Miller
Steve Minnitt • Gary Mitchell • Rosemary Oram • Olive Plant
Margaret Porter • Arthur Robinson • Colin Rock • Pete Rossiter • Sally Roy
Greta Russell* • Graham and Val Scriven • Mary Scriven • Pam Sewell
Audrey Shore* • Ron Skeet • Shirley Sparks • Irene Stimpson • Ron and Guy Tapscott
David Vigar • Gordon Vigar • John Vigar • Joy Vigar • Rita Vigar • Alma Vinter
Lionel Walrond • Charlie and Frances Webb • Edna Webb
Ethel Webb • Rene Winter • Bill Westcott • Stephen Julian Wheadon • Henry Willis

*Now deceased
Abbreviations: WSY – West Somerset Yeomanry; c in front of date – circa (approximately); WI – Women's Institute; YFC – Young Farmers' Club
Illustration facing page: Manor Farm, High Ham at the turn of the century [1]

Foreword

The Parish of High Ham on the Somerset Levels is situated on a high ridge, the slopes of the hill and the low-lying moors below, and includes the villages and hamlets of High Ham, Low Ham, Henley, Paradise, part of Beer and Hamdown. The Parish is remarkable for the large number of residents whose families have lived and farmed here for generations. In living memory there were over 60 farms and smallholdings and a few are still working today. It has been a great pleasure compiling 'A SOMERSET PARISH'. We are grateful to everyone who has generously shared photographs from their albums and given personal accounts of village life from the 1890s up to the 1960s. They are the authors of this book - a first-hand chronicle from a Somerset farming community and a celebration of rural life in the first half of the twentieth century.

Amanda Chuter, Caroline Dickens, Sara Ellis, Viv Hall and Kate Lynch
The High Ham Parish Community Project

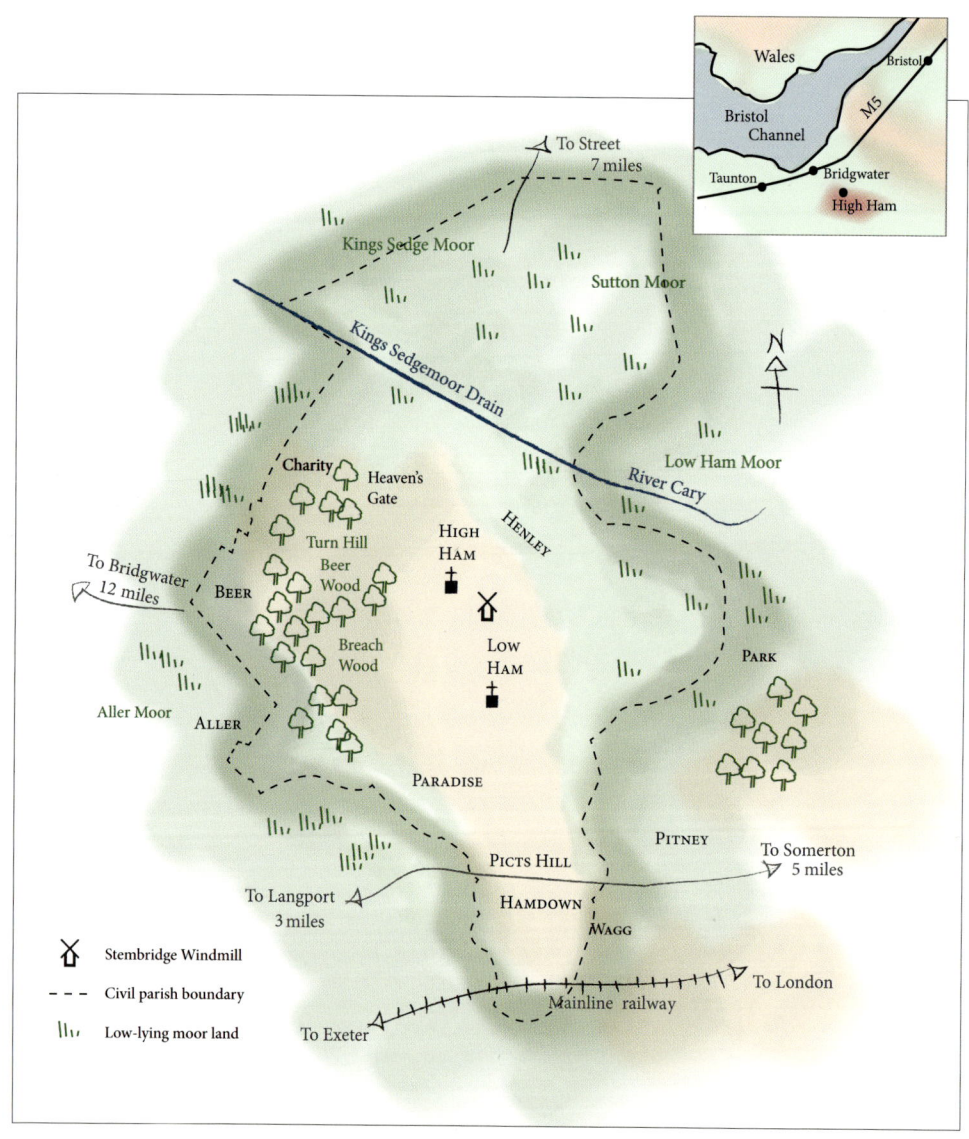

The Parish of High Ham, Somerset

The Turn of The Century

Clockwise from top left: James Skeet (drillsman) at his home at Bramwells, Low Ham, c1900; Addie Matthews' Wedding Day, High Ham Church, 1903; Stawell and Elizabeth Sherrin, Yew Tree Farm, Henley with three of their five children, c1895 (left to right: Edward, Will, Sid) [1]

Clockwise from top left:
Fir Tree Farm, Henley. Austin Lavis, who worked for the Goodings, 1907;
Mr Mathams with older schoolchildren, High Ham School, c1911. Ada Vigar 3rd left, bottom row;
Henry Vigar and his wife Victoria (née Tapscott) of Bridge Farm, Henley, with eight of their ten children. Left to right: Maurice, Florrie, Rose, Daisy, Sid, Molly (Mary Jane), Harold and Ada (between parents), c1909
Will Sherrin [1] of Yew Tree Farm, Henley, c1903;
Fir Tree Farm, Henley, c1907. Sarah and John Gooding with baby daughter Mary (married Percy Williams) and Harold Webb, Sarah's son by her first husband, Hugh Webb (d. 1900). Harold married Ada Vigar.

Henley Corner. Left and right: Elizabeth and Alfred Tapscott, Henry Tapscott's parents, c1910

Clockwise from top left: Florrie, Daisy, Kate and Rose Vigar from Bridge Farm, Henley, c1910

West Somerset Yeomanry annual summer camp, c1910. Middle row, far left: Henry Tapscott (1889-1968) from Henley, father of Ron, Guy and Phyllis

The War Years 1914-18

West Somerset Yeomanry Reservist Camp, Woodbury Common, Exmouth, c1914. 2nd right Henry Tapscott, 7th right Harold Vigar

"My grandfather, Harold Vigar, was only 16 when he joined the West Somerset Yeomanry, you had to be 17 but he put himself down as 16 because he wanted to go to the WSY summer camp at Porlock, it was like a holiday. They rode their horses to Langport West Station and went by train. It was a seaside holiday to them. Anyway, when they were there in 1914 war was declared and they were at the camp, so it backfired a bit, and they had to enlist straightaway. My grandfather went to the Middle East, he was lucky, he had a whale of a time. He was good with horses and he became a sergeant almost straightaway and he was in charge of teaching the other lads to ride - he was away from the start of the war until the end, five years and he never came home in between." Peggy Coombes (née Vigar)

Langport West Station, 1914. Local men of the West Somerset Yeomanry with their horses off to summer camp just before the outbreak of the First World War (Harold Vigar amongst them)

"Father was in the West Somerset Yeomanry, I think he joined in 1908 when he was about 18. A lot of his friends joined too. They used to go on exercises. There was a training camp for a fortnight every year, I think it was at the end of May. They had a lot of fun, it was a bit of a holiday. Then they were called up the moment war broke out. Father was 25. He used to tell us he was on the moor haymaking when someone came with the telegram. He had to report in Bridgwater with his horse straightaway. They were in Bridgwater for a couple of days. All the pubs had places for the horses and they had to stay with their horses, then they were posted to camps." Ron Tapscott

West Somerset Yeomanry (C Squadron) reporting for duty with their horses at Penel Orlieu, Bridgwater, at the outbreak of the First World War. They left from Bridgwater by train on 12 August 1914 to join the rest of the regiment in Winchester. After training in Essex the majority of the regiment left for Gallipoli in September. [1] *"My grandfather, George Ernest Chapman Fisher, was born in 1894 in Bridgwater and was 20 when the war started. He is the third chap from the left in the front row, to the right of the white horse. He took his own horse with him, but it was dead within six weeks. He fought at Passchendaele. When he came home at the end of the war he worked for the council, hauling stone with a horse and cart from the quarries in Street to make roads, then in the 1930s he started farming. He died in 1984."* David Fisher

West Somerset Yeomanry. Artillery training before posting, 1914. Back row 4th and 5th left: Bill Calder, Austin Gooding. Middle row far left: Henry Tapscott. Front row: 1st, 2nd, 3rd left: James Cox, Harold Vigar, Harold Webb (all returned home after the war).

"My dad came to High Ham in about 1912 as groom at Ham Court, then he joined the army in the 1914-18 war and survived that, as many didn't, and married my mother, Bessie Hill. She was a local girl and she became the post lady during the First World War - she took over the job, I think, from three postmen in the village at the start of the war - they all went as soldiers. She had the unfortunate experience of taking most, if not all, the telegrams saying their sons or husbands had been killed. She always related the story of the Mead family down over the hill in Low Ham, that she went with the telegram for one son and then she was there back again within about five days to say the other one was killed, their only children, a tragic occurrence."
Dennis Davis

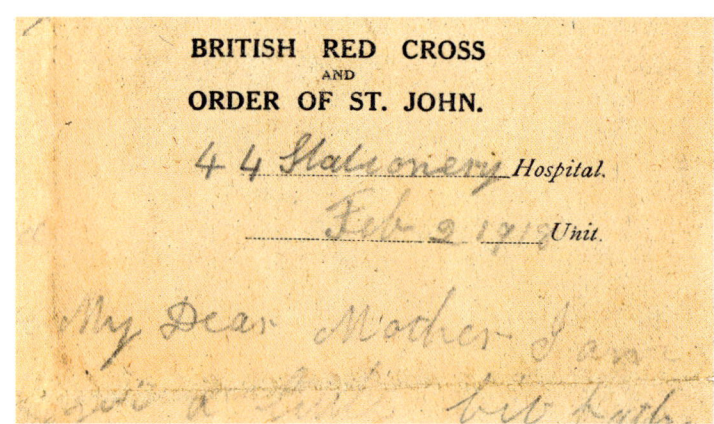

My Dear Mother
I have got a little bit father down the line. The next move I have I shall be in a town. I had a letter from Vigar with two of yours in with it. One was 11 of December, the other the 27. It did seem good to have a letter after so long. I do not get many letters from Beatie but I guess they cannot find me and yet I shall get tons of letters when they find me out. My wound is going on fine now. I am glad to hear that father is keeping so well this winter. I am pleased to hear that you are all in parlour. I suppose that Polly had calf by now. Hope that you have luck with her and that she have a nice calf. You said about give me a egg. I got two for my tea. Would sooner be home for you to nurse me, but I have got a very nice Nurse. I will write to Edward in a day or two. Hope he and Percy is keeping well. I must draw to a close now. With love to all that ask for me and don't forget Uncle Mark. From Sid

Transcript of letter from Sidney Sherrin dated 2 February 1918 from hospital in Cairo. The Sherrin family (parents and five sons) farmed at Yew Tree Farm, Henley. Sidney was on active service with the WSY in Palestine with two of his brothers when he was fatally wounded in December 1917. He died on 17 February 1918. [2]

Bessie Davis (née Hill), High Ham, post lady during the First World War. Photograph taken at School House, High Ham

DIED OF WOUNDS.—Mr. and Mrs. S. Sherrin, of Henley, have received the sad news that their son, Sidney, of the W.S.Y., has died of wounds, received in the fighting in Palestine. The gallant young soldier passed away at Cairo on the 17th inst. Great sympathy is expressed with the bereaved parents, and his fiancee, Miss B. Oram.

Langport Herald, 23 February 1918

118 men from High Ham Parish fought in the First World War, 19 were killed in action and did not return. [3]

Left: William 'Buffer' Ford. Right: Field hospital in the desert in the Dardanelles. William 'Buffer' Ford (top right)

"Mother always told us how Dad was stung by a scorpion and his life was saved when a Turk bit the wound and sucked and spat out the venom. Another story was that when his regiment sailed away from the Dardanelles they believed they were heading for England. When they docked, a soldier called out, 'Where we be to? This isn't **** England!'. Instead of heading home, they were in France! It seems a tragic thing that he came all the way through that war and then was killed by lightning on the farm.

Frank Keevil from Low Ham, was on the front line in France when he saw a horse wounded in No Man's Land. He crawled out to the horse and shot it so that it would not suffer. He received a shot right through the arm. The wound was dressed and then he carried on.

Mother also said that when Hacky Crossman came home from France, he filled a tin bath with water, had a bath, then put his uniform in the used water. In the morning his mother found the surface of the bath water covered in dead lice and fleas. And then there was a story about Hacky walking back from the pub when he was home and Wally Lloyd from Low Ham came up behind him and startled him. Hacky shouted out, 'Don't do that again or I'll kill you!' and he laid Wally out."
Henry Ford

Albert 'Hacky' Crossman

"Father went into the First World War, like lots of the local boys did. I remember him saying that the women had to do a lot of farming work here when the war was on and so many men had gone. Father came home wounded, that's how he came back before the war ended. He had shrapnel in his arm for years, he had a hole in his arm where the bullet went, he lived with it for a long time. Then a man used to come round on a bicycle selling all sorts of ointments, I can remember the man, he had a moustache and a trilby hat, and I remember him saying to Father, 'Try some Salve', and he did and that drew the shrapnel out of his arm, it was marvellous stuff, but you can't get it now. We had the shrapnel in a little jar for years." Frances Webb (née Weech)

Private Henry Charles 'Fred' Cullen from High Ham (7th Battalion, Somerset Light Infantry). He died of his wounds, aged 39, in Varennes Military Hospital, Somme region, France, 17 Feb 1917 and is buried at Varennes Cemetery.

"My father was called up and fought in the First World War. I remember him coming home on leave. He was killed in France. His name was Henry Charles Cullen, but he was always known as Fred, that's what is on the Memorial, Henry Charles 'Fred' Cullen. My mother had six children and she got a war pension, we managed on that. It wasn't too bad." Freda Hayes (née Cullen)

Bryson Bellot, Second Lieutenant North Somerset Yeomanry, in front of Stembridge Mill, High Ham. [4] He died of disease aged 24 in the Somme region 27 March 1918 and is buried at Abbeville Extension Cemetery.

High Ham Brass Band outside the Rectory, 1930s. Ethel Webb recalls that the band used to practice in a barn at Wishell Farm. The band wound up during the Second World War. Left to right. Back row: ?, Tom Oram, Frank Oram, Rev. EBA Hughes, Walter Small, Albert Luxton, Jack Oram, Charles Shepherd. Front row: Maurice Shepherd, Harry Shepherd, Frank Harris, Henry Small, Jack Small, Josie Small.

"The hall in High Ham was built as a memorial to the men who lost their lives during the First World War. [5] It was a barn originally. It was sold to the village and they got a well-known London architect to design it. The chief instigator was Mr. Bellot, he lived in the Windmill, and his son, Bryson, died in the war. The big stone over the fireplace was supplied by the Bellots, but it came from a house somewhere in the South Petherton area. The tall oak panelling came from London. It was always called The Memorial Hall and my father was on the committee from the beginning." Dennis Davis

"I always remember the annual Remembrance Day Service because Father was keen on the British Legion and there used to be a band in the village, the High Ham Brass Band. They used to lead the procession down to the church, but my biggest memory was he used to buy me a chocolate bar in the pub, so that was my big thing, Dad used to buy me a chocolate bar, and I used to run along the Legion marching down to the church. I was born in 1929, so this was probably when I was about six or seven, in the mid-30s. And Dad used to make a laurel wreath with another guy, Ted Priddle, which was placed inside of the church in memorial there. Ted Priddle was in the First World War too with my father." Dennis Davis

Left photo: The Memorial Hall builders. Left to right. Back row: Luther Crossman (Low Ham), mason; Jim Gifford (Low Ham), worker: Oliver Crossman (High Ham), mason; Albert Cullen (High Ham), carpenter; George Church (Low Ham), carpenter; Sam Richards (High Ham), worker. Front row (left to right): Orlando Lavis (High Ham), contractor; Frank Collins (Henley), mason; Orlando Thyer (High Ham), looker-on. Right photo: The Memorial Hall in High Ham, opened in 1925. [6]

Shakespeare at The Court

The cast of A Winter's Tale by William Shakespeare, Ham Court (Daniel Chant with beard far left), 1924

Mr and Mrs Carne-Hill had Ham Court built in the Arts and Crafts style. Mr Carne-Hill died in 1906 just before they were to move in. Elizabeth Carne-Hill lived there for the rest of her life, also managing Court Farm which she owned. From 1919 until the outbreak of the Second World War she hosted annual Shakespearian plays produced by the Mid-Somerset Players in which some locals had small walk-on parts. She also campaigned for piped water, electricity, higher standards in agriculture and nutrition, worked for the Red Cross, started the High Ham Women's Institute and ran a drama group for local children. She died in 1943.[1]

1930s photo of Ham Court

"My father, Ellis Daniel Chant, lived in Stoke-sub-Hamdon. In 1921 he joined the Mid-Somerset Players, who were based in High Ham, as a healing process after the savagery of the First World War. He had been an ambulance driver in Sarajevo. He found the camaraderie of the players stimulating, mixing with actors from all walks of life. I think Mrs Carne-Hill must have been an inspiring woman and I know she also explained the benefits of the Hay Diet to my father, which he took up."
Diana Crossman (née Chant)

"Mrs Carne-Hill had the water put in High Ham. She were always on about water. She used to put on Shakespeare. My husband said he wanted to go to see the theatre, you had to pay to go in, see, I don't suppose it was much, a shilling or sixpence maybe, so he jumped over the wall to see it so they could go in free. Then he said it frightened him to death and he soon came out quicker than he went in, they had spears and things didn't they, it was a Shakespeare play. He said he'd have never gone in if he'd have known it were like that. He'd never seen anything like it I think. He was probably only about six or seven."
Linda Lavis (née Gould)

THE MID-SOMERSET PLAYERS
have produced at
HAM COURT

1919 "A Midsummer Night's Dream."
1920 "Twelfth Night."
1921 "Much Ado about Nothing."
1922 "As You Like It."
1923 "Two Gentlemen of Verona."
1924 "A Winter's Tale."
1925 "Twelfth Night."
1926 "The Rivals."
1927 "All's Well that Ends Well."
1928 "The Merchant of Venice."
1929 "The Fantasticks."
1930 "She Stoops to Conquer."
1931 "The Women have Their Way."
1932 "A Midsummer Night's Dream."
1933 "The Taming of the Shrew."

Performances have also been given at Bath (1926), Bridge House, (1927-8-9), Bridgwater (1927-8-9), Crewkerne (1927), Glastonbury (1927-8), Longleat (1932), Montacute House (1933-4), Martock (1923), South Petherton (1930-1), Stoke-under-Ham (1926), Street (1925), Sydenham Manor (1933), Wells (1932), West Lydford (1930-1), Whitestaunton Manor (1930-1-2-3-4), Wincanton (1922-5-6-9), Yeovil (1924-5).

16th Annual Production
at
HAM COURT

Saturday,
25th August,
1934.

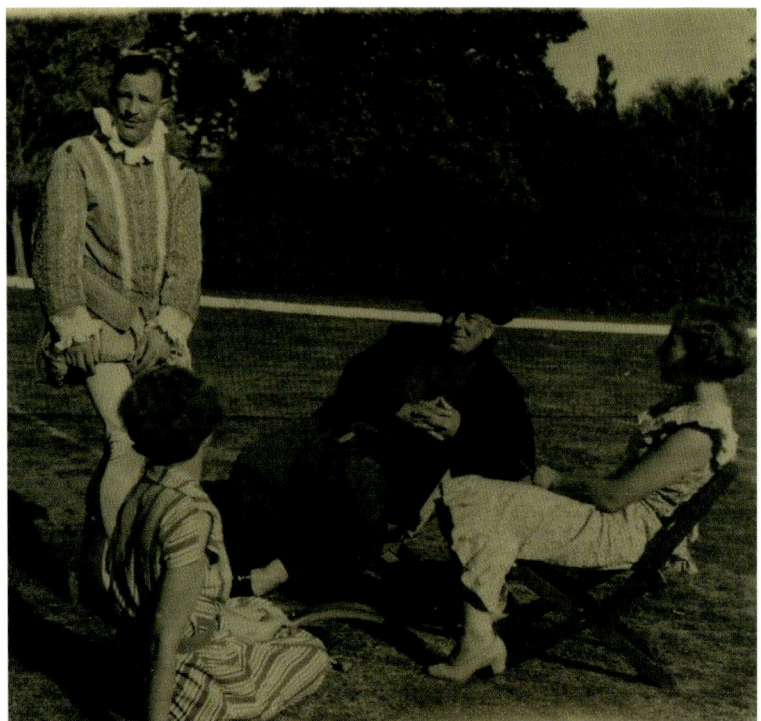

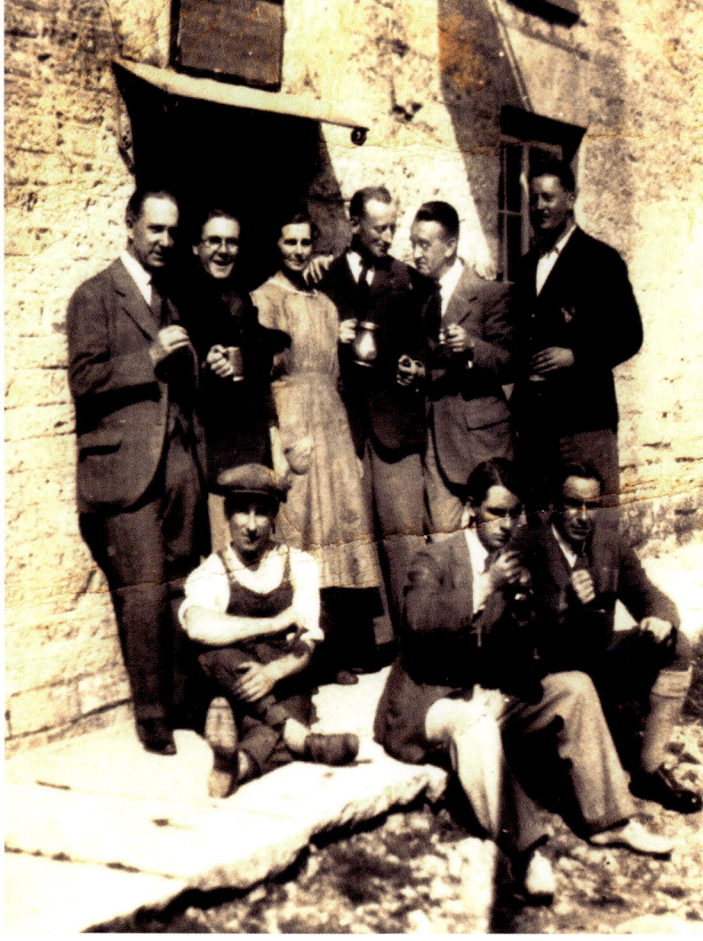

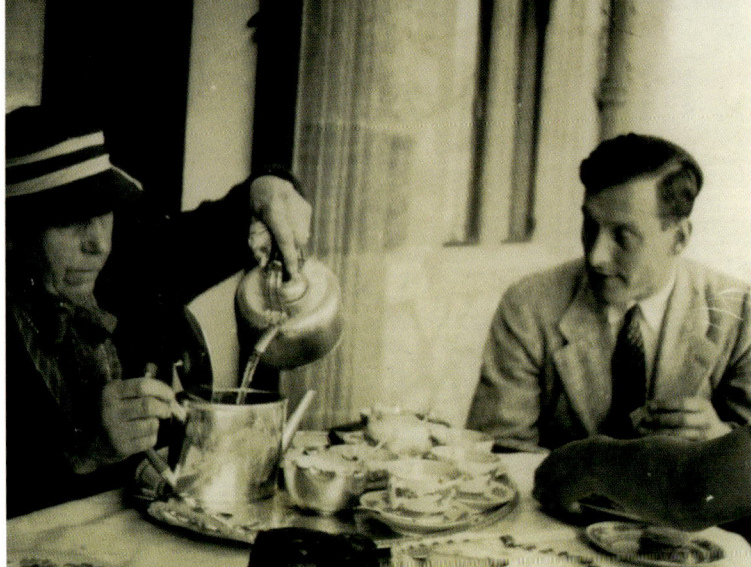

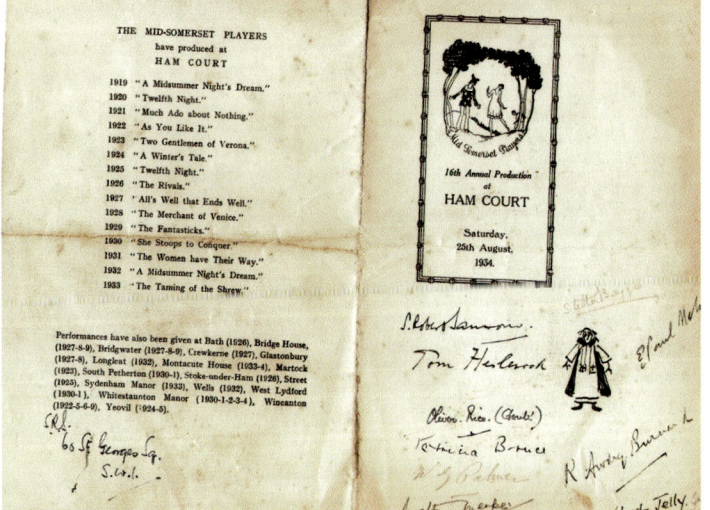

Clockwise from top left:
1920s actors relaxing on the tennis court at Ham Court; Actors drinking at the Kings Head, High Ham, with landlady Mrs Elizabeth Inder. (Daniel Chant seated far right); Signed programme for the 1934 performance by the Mid-Somerset Players (Much Ado About Nothing by William Shakespeare); Mrs Carne-Hill pouring tea at Ham Court, c1934-6.

THE WAR YEARS
1939-45

"The Reverend Hughes borrowed a portable radio to take to church when war was declared. It was quite a rare thing, it was a very modern radio for its time, he borrowed it from Mr and Mrs Hartley who lived in The School House. He had the radio put on the pulpit in the church and at 11 o'clock the congregation listened to Neville Chamberlain declare war on Germany. I was ten at the time, I can remember it being a shock." Dennis Davis

Rosina Hill (known as Rose) at her gate, Hillside Cottage, Fountain, High Ham (now Hogweed Cottage). This was where Irene Stimpson stayed. Rose Hill lived there until the mid-1940s.

"I came out of London at the start of the war with my mother and aunt and baby cousin, and we stayed with an old lady who was a relation. I was six. The cottage we lived in was just above the farm owned by Mr and Mrs England. They had a dreadful cockerel, it would go for anybody walking past the farm entrance. I would be taken milking in a pony and trap and one evening I can remember sitting one side of the big range with a tiny medicine glass of home-made cider with Mr England sitting the other side with a much larger glass. The little cottage we stayed in had a thatched roof and the windows were so low that my mother could lean out of her bedroom window and collect the post from the postman. There was no electricity, only oil lamps. I can remember the old lady standing on the settle and lighting the lamp." Irene Stimpson (neé Figg)

Detail from High Ham School photo, 1939 (see page 64), Irene Stimpson seated centre

"When I first had the children we had a tied cottage, my husband was a farm labourer, we had evacuees there. We had a baby and a mother and we couldn't get a bed for love nor money, they had to sleep on straw. My husband said, 'If you can get some blankets, I'll get some straw.' It made a lovely bed, they were happy as anything."
Linda Lavis (née Gould)

"I was evacuated from London and arrived in Low Ham on 26 October 1940, I was seven years old. I made friends and the Somerset children always made us welcome, we just became part of the school. That first night when I arrived I was in a room on my own, it was dark, there was no electricity, I was so frightened, and I kept calling out. Poor Mrs Hill, she had to light a candle and come in, she had an 18 month old daughter, Shirley. She was really nice to me from the beginning. After that I soon felt at home, although it was terrifying when the German bombers used to go overhead, they were going to Swansea and Yeovil. It was a shock going from London to the country, there was no water in the house and no inside toilet. Mrs Hill was always very kind and my gran and aunts and uncles visited. I didn't want to to leave when I had to go back to London, I wanted to stay, it wasn't easy going back."
Alma Vinter (née Willoughby)

Alma Vinter with Granny Scriven

"I was evacuated with my sister from Leeds to the Rectory, High Ham, for the first eight or nine months of the war. The garden was looked after by Edward Priddle, a good friend to us children. Across The Green at the village shop, kept by Mr and Mrs Hunt, my sister and I spent pocket money on liquorice bootlaces."
Arthur Robinson, grandson of Rev EBA Hughes (Rector of St. Andrew's, High Ham 1927-1942)

Jack Lavis pulling a cart with evacuees

Watercolour painting by Ronald Gray dated 1948 [1]
The painting is of a thatched cottage in High Ham (since demolished) on the corner of Windmill Road and Field Road. In the distance is The Old Cobblers.

"During the war my mother had a paying guest, he was Ronnie Gray, a watercolour painter. From time to time he used to have quite famous people come to see him, people such as Augustus John and Wilson Steer and Alexander Fleming who discovered penicillin. They stayed in my bedroom and I had to go in with my parents. Yes, Augustus John came and stayed in my bedroom and Ronnie Gray said, 'If he's coming again I'm going to get him to give you a picture', which he did, but we could never find it, I don't know what my mother did with it, but we never found it. I can remember the picture. Augustus John had a beard and Wilson Steer was a little smart bow-tie man." Dennis Davies

Pilot who landed in Paradise!

I WAS born and lived in Somerset at a place called Paradise Mill, Langport, until coming to Worksop in 1947. I recall this incident quite clearly in 1942:

The German bombers and fighters were flying overhead and were being intercepted by our brave Spitfire pilots, one of whom was unfortunately hit, causing the pilot to bail out.

He landed in our orchard at the back of our house. He managed to find his way to our front door and woke me up at about 3 am.

After telling me what had happened, and after I tended a big gash on his leg which he sustained by catching it on the wing of his 'plane as he jumped out, he asked me where he was. I immediately told him he had landed in Paradise, to which he promptly replied: "I really thought I was on my way there when I got hit."

He had also lost his flying boots as he descended, so I lent him a pair of plimsoles, which he promised he would return.

The shoes never arrived, and it was a standing joke whenever a plane flew over: "I wonder if that pilot is wearing my plimsoles."

After having made him comfortable and giving him a cup of tea, he asked to be taken to the nearest telephone. So I took him to my nearest neighbour who had a 'phone, who was the then famous band leader of radio, Mr Hugo Rignald.

His first words to me and the pilot when we finally aroused him were, "Are you British?", as I could have been misled and probably have been helping the enemy in disguise. Everything turned out all right and we managed to get through to the pilot's airbase at Bath.

While we were 'phoning, the police were tapping telephone calls as they knew an aeroplane had crashed. They were soon on the scene, much to my sorrow, as I was hoping to go into our orchard and collect some of the silk parachute to make some clothes as we were on rations for clothes in those days!

JOAN SPEARING

Squadron Leader Robin McNair (1918-1996), the pilot who landed in Paradise

On the night of 25 April 1942, 87 Squadron based at Charmy Down near Bath, was on patrol to intercept German night raids on Bath, Bristol and Swansea. One of the planes, a Hurricane BE566 flown by Robin McNair, was orbiting local searchlight batteries in the hope of a raider being illuminated when the need to change petrol tanks arose. When another tank was selected the engine would not pick up and McNair had no alternative but to bail out. As he evacuated the plane, his parachute did not deploy properly, but by wrestling with the lines he managed to get it open just before hitting the ground (which would account for his first words to Joan Spearing!). His Hurricane went on to crash outside Somerton, now Fevin Nature Reserve Burial Site, Westcombe. McNair's other war service included: The Battle of Britain, night fighter operations during the German Blitz, the Dieppe raid, D-Day and sorties against V-1 rocket sites. (This information has come to light from Robin McNair's obituary in The Independent, the Hurrricane BE566 Accident Card and 'A Flying Life' by John Maynard).

"My Dad and Herb Cook, from up the farm (Netherham), they were on Home Guard duty that night. A stick of bombs were dropped and one landed on a cottage in Low Ham.[2] Dad and Mr Cook had to go down and go into the cottage that was bombed. It was Mr Church's. Dad had to go up the rickety stairs 'cos Mr Church was in bed. Mr Church had some of his fingers blown off, I don't know how many. They took him to hospital. Ted Church was only a baby but they brought him down. I do remember that for years and years nobody did anything to that cottage, all overgrown with brambles, but it had the most wonderful wild sweet-pea in the garden, just beautiful.
Dad rented a small plot of land down the road. We called it 'The Orchard'. He kept pigs to supplement our family income. We all used to go down there and feed them. We kept a few chickens as well. There was a huge pond just behind where my brother built his house. There were these dips all in a row across the bottom of what we call the Golf Links.[3] This is where they off-loaded their bombs that night. We had a big crater in the orchard."
Gwen Chubb (née Bown)

"I can remember the aeroplanes going over at night to Bristol, to bomb Bristol." Edna Webb (née Sherrin)

"They had bombing down Low Ham. When this happened I hadn't gone to work in Westlands, I was still down Langport working. We heard they had dropped a bomb the other side of Low Ham Chapel. 'Course my parents lived that side, I was worried stiff till I heard they were alright. You couldn't pick the phone up and ask them. There was no phone to do it with. I suppose some people had phones then but I didn't know them."
Frances Webb (née Weech)

626 Squadron, Wickenby, Lincolnshire, January/ February 1944
Left to right: J. Colles, Wireless Operator; W. Mair, Navigator; L. Smith 'Smithy', Mid Upper Gunner; Jimmy Stewart, Pilot; S. Wilson, Engineer; Len Wilson, Bomb Aimer; Gordon Vigar, Rear Gunner

"I volunteered to go in the Air Force as soon as I could when my time came. I needn't have gone because of the farm. I flew on 32 operations, I was the rear gunner. This was taken just before leaving for Berlin one night - we were stationed at Wickenby in Lincolnshire, it's a Lancaster, it was January or February 1944, I was 20. I think we went to Berlin about 15 times, that was a normal night. They used to tell us not to look down because it would ruin our night vision. We often came back with holes in the aeroplane. That's Jimmy Stewart, the pilot in the middle, that's me on the right. After the war I came back to the family farm here in Henley." Gordon Vigar

The Low Ham Searchlight

"It was a searchlight with a gun and it was to protect Yeovilton. If it was a quiet night, if there was no fear of bombs coming over, just sometimes they trained the light on my brothers' bedroom, it was in the back, and Fred and Andrew used to snigger that they'd been able to read their comics. I don't think it happened often and maybe for only ten minutes, but we used to laugh! The searchlight was operated by soldiers, there was a whole barrack of them and they stayed up at the top of Cook's Hill. There's still a Nissen hut there now, I think it should be preserved. All the other buildings have fallen down. One of the soldiers used to mend our shoes, he used to get rubber from the tyres. His wife came and stayed with Mum. We are still in touch."
Rita Vigar (née Ford)

Soldiers in back of jeep passing Glastonbury Tor. Drawing by Stanley Lewis[4]

Drawings by Stanley Lewis of Low Ham camp, situated at the top of Cook's Hill, where the searchlight crew was billeted. Top: Soldiers camouflage-painting the Nissen huts. The goat was the regimental mascot and kept the grass under control. Bottom: Soldiers resting, Low Ham camp

"The Low Ham searchlight was sited at the bottom of Cook's Hill at Ivy Corner, where there is a sharp right. On the bend there is a gate where there was a pond and a field beyond. The light was sited in some old ruins. My mother told us that one group of soldiers who manned the searchlight moved on from Low Ham to a site on the east coast and when they were on duty they were all killed." Henry Ford

A humorous picture by Stanley Lewis showing him painting the searchlight at Low Ham for The Gloucester Regiment with fellow soldiers looking on

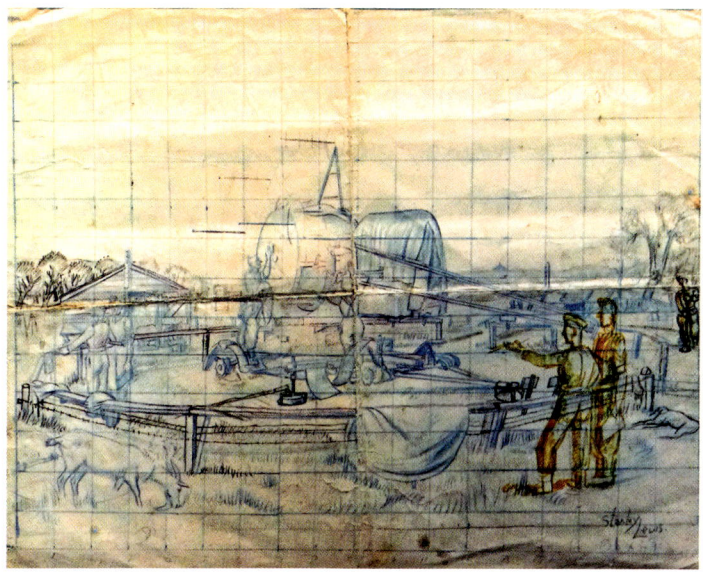

Working drawing for canvas painting of the Low Ham Searchlight by Stanley Lewis. The finished painting measured approx. 22 x 36" and was painted in 1943. Every member of the crew was incorporated. It was framed and hung in the Officers' Mess for a time. Despite attempts by the late Stanley Lewis and his family, the finished painting has not, to date, been traced.

"Lieutenant Colonel MacWaters was in charge and he interviewed me concerning painting a picture commemorating the searchlight service during the war. He gave me a list of 15 possible subjects for me to choose from and I chose Morning Maintenance on a Searchlight Site. He allowed a jeep with a driver to travel to different sites to choose a suitable location for the picture. Eventually I chose a site at Low Ham in Somerset. This site was most suitable as the great searchlight was situated in a Somerset apple orchard and looking north was the famous Glastonbury Tor. I settled there and became one of the searchlight team and in my spare time I worked on the painting."
From a letter written by Stanley Lewis [4]

"I remember lorries bringing timber to the Golf Links[3] during the war. The Yanks were billed at the egg packing station, what had been the workhouse [5], where Hamdown Court is now. There were prisoners there and there was a big shed on the Golf Links where I heard they were making equipment for D Day. They used to march the men out from the egg packing factory with loads of timber. There were other soldiers who were billeted in huts at the top of the hill, they were manning the searchlight, you can still see a hut there now. I was a boy and we used to go down and play football with the soldiers. Once we went down on a Sunday morning, but Lionel Cook wouldn't allow us to play football on a Sunday and we had to pack it in." Dennis Davis

The Home Guard

"I can remember Father telling us for ages they only had brush or broom handles for guns and to get around they only had bicycles. They used to meet in the Cottage on the Green. Mr Clark, who was senior to them, used to check up on them. They would have the fire going, or be having a brew or playing cards. When they heard him coming they would jump out the window at the back and go on patrol! They used to practice marching on the green and down by the school. Father and Brian Vigar, when they were out on patrol, used to take their own guns as well and go rabbiting. They used to sell them at Prideaux for sixpence each. They used to guard the train-line bridges around Somerton when the ammunition trains were going through late at night. Father said they were on guard duty many a night through and then had to come home and work on the farm milking and that."
Margaret Porter (née Webb)

Members of the High Ham Home Guard outside the High Ham Memorial Hall (this photograph is the only known record)
Left to right. Back row: Ray Reading, Hubert Priddle, Norman Crossman, Jack Cullen, Maurice Gould, Harry Johnson, Albert Cullen, Maurice Hurd, Jeff Oram, Ted Gould, Austin Lavis. Middle row: Vigar Webb, Charlie Scriven, Bill Richards, Sid Vigar, Sid Langford, Henry Vigar, Ed Brooks. Front row: Ron Tapscott, David Coombes, Sgt. Fred Clark, Henry Crocker, Ken Duddridge, Percy Windsor, Gordon Vigar, Sid Shepherd [6]

"Dad was in the Home Guard before he volunteered to go in the Air Force and became a rear gunner. He did tell us a few stories about when they were in the Home Guard. They used the weathervane on top of the church as a target and used to shoot at it to try to make it go round, Simon Spearing (who had the shop) knocked its head off, it still hasn't got a head on it today. It's quite funny because Simon Spearing became a Church Warden later! Then there was another story about when they used to patrol Langport and through Kelways bulb fields and Dad said that the Home Guard always had the best looking gardens at home, they were full of really nice bulbs!" David Vigar

HOME-MADE SYREN

In the absence of official instructions regarding air-raid warnings, the Wardens at Low Ham, a Somerset village with a population of no more than 100 people, have devised a scheme of warning, which they claim—and with some justification—is most effective. Mr G. A. Goodfellow (an engineer) and his son (an electrician) have between them provided a simple electrical apparatus by which a signal can be radiated at the shortest possible notice. It makes use of a motor horn erected on a mast, and the blasts can be operated by an ordinary press-button switch. The experiments carried out have proved entirely satisfactory to the local wardens, an intermittent signal being introduced as a warning and a long blast of one minute's duration being employed for "all clear." Observers presented reports that the warning could be heard distinctly in all parts of the village and in other places outside. The apparatus is not by any means costly, and can be run from a motor-car accumulator. The system has not been approved by the local authority, but the inventors and others do not see why it should not be

Western Gazette 1 September 1939

"I used to clean my brother Vigar's brass buttons and his boots for the Home Guard. He was in a reserved occupation. Father was an ARP warden. He had a navy blue coat and a tin hat. It was a rush when they went on parade on Sundays. They would muster at the King's Head, march down to the church, go to church, march back and disperse - into the pub!" Rene Winter (née Webb)

"I was a messenger for the Home Guard. They had several weekends of manoeuvres and I went from camp to camp on a bicycle. The message usually said, 'All's well'. It sounds quite funny doesn't it. But of course had there been an invasion it would have been important to have a girl like me, who wasn't suspicious, taking messages, I had to keep the message in a wallet round my neck." Peggy Coombes (née Vigar)

"Brian was about 13 when the war broke out, and then he wanted to join up when he was old enough. His older brother, Gordon, was in the Air Force, but his father said, 'If you go there'll be no farm left'. There was a great drive to feed people and farming was important and it was a reserved occupation. Anyway, he was in the Home Guard and he and Vigar used to have some good stories about their time guarding the ventilation shaft on Somerton Hill." [6] Rita Vigar (née Ford)

Drawing of hut on the searchlight by Stanley Lewis

"Father worked up the forestry at Bowdens and Breach Wood. He had a pony and cart to get up there. It was all dirt tracks and all dark because it was mainly fir trees. All up the other one it was all beech trees. They cut all the big stuff for rifle butts. They collared all the walnut trees, lovely walnut trees we had. They cut them all down for the war. My brother worked up at Bowdens. There was a big contract to cut down all the big stuff for the war. There wasn't chain saws, it was all crosscut saws and axes." Charlie Webb

Everyday Life 1939-1945

"I remember the terrible storm in 1942 when Mr Ford was struck by lightning, that was a terrible thing. They called him Buffer. When he was killed he was just teaching us how to ride a bike. There were barns opposite the house, there's a house there now, but there were wagons in the barns and we used to play mums and dads and hospitals there. Mrs Ford sold cigarettes and we used to go behind the hay rick and have a puff. It put me off - I never smoked since."
Alma Vinter (née Willoughby)

Amy Ford and her seven children, Gares Cottage, Low Ham (with Gold Flake sign [7]), 1946. Left to right. Back: Nora, Fred, Alma. Middle: Vera, Rita, Amy. Front: Henry, Andrew

"Our father was William Ford, he was known as 'Buffer' because of the sound of the steam engine he drove. He drove Keevil Brothers' steam threshing machines. He was in the First World War in Palestine, he came right through the war. After the war he married Amy Crossman and had seven children, then in 1942 he was struck by lightning where they were working in Keevils' yard. It began to rain and they didn't have time to put the wimsheet [8] over the ricks, and they all sheltered in between the two ricks. Father was struck and died. Then our mother, Amy Ford, had seven children to bring up. Everyone helped and she worked doing anything she could. She sold cigarettes, we had a Gold Flake sign on the house. Soldiers who were stationed at the searchlight used to come and buy their cigarettes." Rita Vigar (née Ford)

"I joined the YFC when I was 16, we would meet in Langport. One time in the summer, it was double summer time during the war, when we were all going home, we were stopped by Sergeant Waites, the local policeman, wanting to know where we were all going at this time of night. 'Home', we all said (there were about 30 of us on our bicycles). 'Where's that?' he said. 'Pitney, High Ham, Aller, Somerton, Pedwell, Ashcott, Littleton, Keinton, Compton', we replied. He was a bit taken aback from all that, so then, so as not to lose face, he told us that it would be lighting-up time in ten minutes. 'So you'd better get off home quick!' he said and cycled off." Joy Vigar (née Sherrin)

"Jam-making sessions took place in High Ham village hall when fruit was available. Water was taken in churns to the hall and WI members arrived armed with oil stoves, knives, preserving pans, wooden spoons and aprons. One member pushed her apparatus along the village road in her wheelbarrow. Ministry of Food regulations were very strict and exact quantities of sugar, water and fruit had to be used and boiled down. Members sat, each by her own oil stove, stirring away in increasing heat and hilarity."
From 'Somerset Remembers, Recollections of Country People' compiled by the Somerset Federation of Women's Institutes

"In the winter of 1945-6 I was on leave and went to the pub and Jo Hurd tapped me on the shoulder. 'Don't go away', he said, and he told me to wait and at one o'clock in the morning four of us went off to the churchyard. The bier was there over the wall, what they carried the coffins on, and we got it and took it off to his place, that's called Rose Cottage now. The pig was there cut up. We loaded the bier up with pig meat, then brought it up to Maggie Barnard's House, the narrow house behind the church. They were engaged for years. You had to have a licence if you killed a pig, you had to give up your coupons if you did, and that pig that night wasn't legally killed, so Jo walked in front in the dark to see if anyone was coming. There was no policeman in the village then, they went before the war, it wouldn't have made any difference I don't think. There were three of us pulling or pushing. We really enjoyed that. Oh that was a night that was!" Ron Tapscott

Left to right: Ron, Lily (mother), Henry (father), Guy and Phyllis Tapscott. Ron was in the Home Guard at this time, working in a reserved occupation on the farm, later he volunteered to train in the Air Force.

"During the war on Saturday afternoons we used to meet in Henley Hall. Dad used to take me down in the pony and trap. We used to do plays, charades, a bit of drama, singing and dancing. Things like that. We put on concerts for parents." Joy Vigar (née Sherrin)

"I can remember during the war one of our neighbours could never get enough sugar. My family didn't eat much sugar, none of us took sugar in tea, still don't, I don't know how it happened. My mum used to have a bag of sugar left over sometimes, it was rationed. My mother's friend, she'd come up and say, 'Ame, have you got any sugar for I?' and they didn't buy it, we swapped things in those days, it worked fine."
Nora Langford (née Ford)

"I had my 21st birthday down Taunton in the army. Cold water, shaving outside in the frosts. Didn't come home, went straight into the war and didn't come out till 1946." Charlie Webb

"When the war finished I was still up at Westlands. They didn't want the planes so I went in the experimental office before I left, but I would rather have been out in the shop working. When the war finished all the married women working were sacked straightaway. They only kept the single ones on and 'course when I got married I couldn't stay. The men wanted their jobs back. When Charlie came back from the army within two months we were married. We lived at Upton with Charlie's sister. We had part of the house - you couldn't get a house in those days." Frances Webb (née Weech)

The Welcome Home Float, High Ham Grand Carnival in aid of the Welcome Home Fund, 8 September 1945

The Welcome Home Grand Carnival 8 September 1945

"We used to do things for the War Effort during the war, but there weren't any carnivals, they were stopped. Then at the end of the war there was a big celebration. The procession started from the village hall. A lot of the people came and dressed up in their costumes at the hall. Then we processed down through The Green and out to the fields on Windmill Road. There was a big committee, and two or three members organised the different sections like the horse show and the dog show. One man came from Isle Brewers and Ted Gould from Court Farm, he showed his horse, he was the son of Bert Gould, who was down at New Road Farm. The 'Park Rovers' float had all people who lived at Park on it, with Henry leading the horse. In the carnival procession there was a man in fancy dress on a horse, he was in front of me. Joe Small, he dressed up as a nurse, he used to play in the band." Joy Vigar (née Sherrin)

The Welcome Home Grand Carnival, 8 September 1945

The Low Ham Roman Villa

"The discovery of the Low Ham mosaic is the story of a series of fortuitous events. They began with the death of a sheep belonging to Herbert Cook in 1937. Herbert chose to bury the sheep where it lay. In the process he discovered a fragment of tile that he felt might be of historic interest. It is about the size of a hand, flat and with a combed pattern on one side. On a visit to Taunton, Herbert took the tile to the Somerset County Museum where it was identified as part of a box flue tile from a Roman central heating system. The tile was given to the Museum and a note about it was published in the Proceedings of the Somerset Archaeological and Natural History Society. This would have been the end of the story were it not for the fact that in 1945 the young Lionel Walrond, who lived in nearby Pitney, and had already developed a keen interest in Roman antiquities, read about the tile. Intrigued, he got permission to carry out a small excavation. More tile fragments were discovered indicating the probable existence of a Roman villa. Later that summer a small team was brought together to excavate on a larger scale." Steve Minnitt, Museum of Somerset

Left to right: Lionel Walrond, Herbert Cook, David Walrond, Bob Scriven, Harry Webb and Charlie Scriven standing by the heating system which was below the floor of one of the warm rooms in the Low Ham Roman villa's bathing suite (the mosaic was not above the heating system). Lionel discovered the mosaic, Herbert was the farmer on whose land the villa was found, David is Lionel's cousin and along with local men, Bob, Harry and Charlie, helped with the archaeological dig.

"We dug a hole six feet by three feet... we obviously dug carefully, we were going through building debris, then we came down on a layer of roof tiles and underneath the layer of roof tiles was a layer of painted plaster but all of that had rotted away and become a soft mortary muddle, and then it was dinnertime, so we sat on the side of the trench with our feet dangling inside and said, 'Now let's just think'. And I can remember that Stephen Dewar said, 'Oh terrible disappointment, worked so hard to uncover all this and all we find is just a single stone flag floor'. Well that word 'flag floor' stuck in my mind. Our trench was six feet by three feet and usually the biggest flagstone you would find in the Langport and Pitney area would have been about three feet by two feet, so why were there no joins between the flagstones? And I looked and I looked, and by that time the breeze was starting to dry out a little tiny bit of the surface and I saw some small white flecks and those flecks that I saw were the ones beyond the first of the riders, just behind his cloak and before you come to the head of the second horse, so I got a little scraping tool and I got down onto my knees and scraped away with it... I scraped away about nearly a tenth of an inch of lime, just as you get inside a kettle, grey and quite hard... so that was the first spot that came to light and I can remember turning round and saying, 'It's not flagstones, it's tesserae!'. Immediately everyone put down the last remains of their cups of tea and came down with spades and scrapers and trowels and all sorts of things and uncovered a part of the horse, a part of the second rider, and the border behind... and I knew we had found something important...

We had two teams of diggers working independently, a daytime team and an evening team, underneath the control of the visiting Director. The pavement itself was open for three seasons and while the mosaic was uncovered we had lots of visitors every day of the week, but more on Sundays - even Sir Victor and Lady Bonham Carter came with a couple of other people who later became Members of Parliament, and General Smuts, the South African Prime Minister. It stayed open in the evenings, often until 11 o'clock at night, because we had double summer time and so the evenings were very, very light and so it would be 11 o'clock before some of those people began to walk back across the fields. It was a very short sleeping time because we had to be up at about half past six the next morning to get the milk ready, but nevertheless it was wonderful fun." Lionel Walrond
(from a talk given at the Museum of Somerset on 6 November 2013)

A visit to the archaeological dig by the Somerset Archaeological and Natural History Society on 13 August 1947

The Low Ham Roman Mosaic

"The mosaic records the tragic love story of Dido and Aeneas, as written by the Roman poet Virgil in the 1st century BC and is told in five narrative panels: 1.(Left) Aeneas is on a god-ordained mission to found Rome. His journey is interrupted when a storm forces his ships to land at Carthage on the coast of North Africa. Gifts, including a jewelled diadem, are offered to Dido, Queen of Carthage. 2. (Bottom) The main characters in the story are shown in this panel. They are (left to right): Aeneas, Cupid (disguised as Aeneas's son, Ascanius), Venus (goddess of love and mother of Aeneas) and Queen Dido. 3. (Right) Venus has been plotting to make Dido and Aeneas fall in love. She intends this to happen during a hunt. Cupid leads the way. Aeneas is clearly thinking more about Dido than the hunt! 4. (Top) A storm arranged by Venus disrupts the hunting party. Dido and Aeneas take shelter under the trees and their love affair begins. 5. The central panel shows Venus between two cupids, each holding a torch. One torch points downwards to represent the tragic death of Dido. She killed herself when Aeneas left Carthage to continue his journey. The other torch points upwards and symbolises Aeneas as the founder of the Roman people." Steve Minnitt, Museum of Somerset

Two pages from the book signed by over 8,000 people who visited the Low Ham mosaic while it was uncovered between 1946 and 1947

"There was considerable interest in the discovery and the site was visited by over 8,000 people in 1946 and 1947. The excavations, together with more recent air photographs, show the mosaic to have been the floor of a room in the bath block of an especially large courtyard villa. The mosaic, which dates to about AD 350, was to remain in situ until September 1953. With the land owner's agreement and with funding in place, it was carefully rolled up in seven sections and taken to Bristol where the panels were laid upon reinforced concrete. Later that year it was delivered to the Somerset County Museum where it has been on public display ever since. Today it is one of the star objects in the recently refurbished Museum of Somerset."
Steve Minnitt, Museum of Somerset

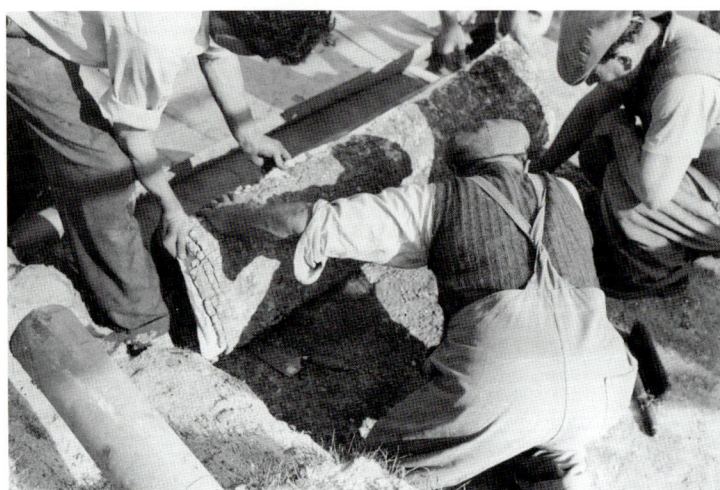

Clockwise from top left:
Front page Illustrated London News Saturday May 11, 1946; the 1946 excavation; two views of the lifting of the mosaic in September 1953

High Days and Holidays

Clockwise from top: Heavy Horse Show, 1940s; Bessie Davis in costume for Shakespearian play at Ham Court, 1920s; High Ham School Pageant, c1912; Henley Sunday School outing, c1922; Darts Team, Kings Head 1950s; Low Ham entry 'Wagon Train', Langport Carnival, 17 July 1965; Mark Hurd (1859-1931) wearing Club sash on Club Day; Edwin Henry Fouracre (see page 106 and footnote); carol singing in Henley

Club Day

'Ov all the year round, dye know,
The girtest, grandest day,
Amongst us simple country volk,
Is twenty ninth of May.
Ther's harvest whom an Christmas time,
But taint no good to talk,
The grandest day we do know,
Is when our club do know,
Is when our club do walk.' [1]

High Ham Women's Benefit Society, [2] c1900, High Ham Rectory. Left to right. Back: Lucy Oram (2nd), Milly Fido (7th); middle: Jane Ford (10th), Elizabeth Cullen (11th) Martha Bartlett (13th), with Dr Johnson and dog

High Ham Club members outside High Ham School on Club Day, c1900. Friendly Societies (often know as Clubs) traditionally paraded once a year.[3]

"Club members paid in so much a month, sixpence or something like that, it was put in the bank, invested, and perhaps after five years the interest was divided up equally amongst them. If a man died who belonged to the club, then all the others would pay a shilling to the widow, a shilling each, and if any member lost his wife the other members would pay sixpence. This was when I was a boy in the 1920s. The club members met once a year on The Green, that was Club Day. They paraded around and stopped at four or five places for sandwiches and cider. There was a club banner at the front and the High Ham band played. They attended a church service, then they had a meal at the school. Mrs Perrin, who lived opposite, cooked it. The food was carried over to the school and kept warm on an oil stove. As it was Whit Tuesday, the school was closed and could be used. They'd go round to the villages, pick up a sandwich here and a glass of cider there, and at the end of the day they could certainly show you how to dance!"
Ron Tapscott

Club Day, 25 May 1920. Bell-ringers, St. Andrew's, High Ham.
Left to right: Hayman Scriven, Joe Hurd, William and Fred Crossman, Arthur Scriven (boy)

Club Day outing, 1920s. Far left: William and Bert Wheadon. One of the club members is holding a ceremonial stave that was carried at club events and the annual 'walk' on Club Day.

Club Day, 7 June 1927. William 'Buffer' Ford and Mrs Frances Scriven, wife of Hayman

"At the top of Stout, in a field on the right, a beer tent was erected. There was also a tent where the women drank tea. The main attraction on the field was a fight. There was a bit of racing for the children and an egg-and-spoon race for the ladies. They were probably over 60, but they all looked old as I was only six or seven. They went to Vile Sherrin at Manor Farm for the cider. He drew the cider into a bucket and used a jug to fill up the glasses. When most of the men had gone on their way there was always a few left and Vile would ask them if they would like some more. 'Yes!' They were real scrumpers, no interest in the band and club, just the cider. Then he put the jollop in the bucket, a product of the root mirabalis, a fierce laxative! Then someone put barbed wire on the gate. One man broke his trousers getting over. Some men had to go home as the jollop had worked! It was very funny." Ron Tapscott

Club Day, 7 June 1927. Left to right: Hayman Scriven, Henry Cox, Joe Fisher, J. Hill, William 'Buffer' Ford, J. Cox

Club Day, 7 June 1927. High Ham and Henley Band at Keevils, Low Ham

Low Ham, 1928 Club Day. The union flag, topped by a garland of flowers, is held by Henry Small.

Brass stave heads used by two of High Ham's Clubs [4]

Outings

"In the photograph it is my mother, Elizabeth Cullen, standing in the middle wearing the large white motoring veil. My grandmother, Jane Ford, is the woman in the bonnet and dark coat standing at the back on the far left. It was a great day to go to Cheddar. I remember it very well, I think it was a Women's Institute outing, about 1924. I'm the young girl seated last on the left without a hat and my sister Louie is sitting on the driver's right. There weren't many days out. Mostly everything happened in the village." Freda Hayes (née Cullen)

"We didn't go far on the outings, not usually, even Weston and Weymouth were a very long way - so far you almost took pyjamas! None of the kids liked Burnham, there was no Woolworths there! You could go in Woolworths for free, it was a good place, oh the finest place in the world - Weston had one, but Burnham didn't. You could go in there if it rained. We didn't have any money much in the 1920s and 30s - I remember one year we had eighteen pence and that was a fortune, old money, one shilling and sixpence… three pints of beer, sixpence a pint, but I can assure you we never had much beer!" Ron Tapscott

Top: High Ham outing to Cheddar Caves, c1924. As well as family members identified by Freda Hayes, Bessie Davis is seated above the X.
Bottom: Henley Chapel Sunday School Outing to Cheddar Caves, 1922/3. Boy held up is Ron Tapscott.

"BIBBY" coaches leaving the Tunnel exit at Birkenhead

"I can't remember if we paid. I expect we paid a bit. But they (Bibby's) [5] *organised it all. It was in the 1950s, they took us up by coach and we went round their factory in Liverpool and also Levers soap factory. In the evening they took us to see Blackpool illuminations. We stayed in a hotel in Southport."* Ethel Webb

Henley Chapel Sunday School outing, c1958. Left to right. Back: Mrs Cook, Margaret Cullen, Molly Cook, Edna Martin, Mrs Cullen, Pearl Clark, Mary Foster, Maureen Scriven. Front: Michael Clark, Mrs Crawley, Richard Webb

"We used to all meet on the green at Henley and when we got the coach every child that got on Mr John Oram gave us half a crown (twelve and a half pence) to spend. We went to Weymouth. They used to say if you got lost go back under the clock and wait. When we went the village would sit in a row on deck chairs on the sand and you could go down to the sea and you could see your pile of stuff because you were all together. You could go into town and leave your bags and everything because the others would look to it. We'd perhaps go to Woolworths. Everything was a shilling (five pence). The Punch and Judy was there and the sandcastle man." Ethel Webb

"The British Legion used to have an annual outing, we had at least two coachfuls and they used to set off with barrels of cider and the bus went a few miles and then it had to stop because somebody wanted to relieve themselves, but of course what they really wanted was to drink, so by the time they arrived half of them were quite merry." Dennis Davis

Women's Institute and British Legion

"Mrs Carne-Hill founded the Women's Institute in 1920. The first meeting was at The Court. The rest of the meetings were in the Dairy Hut at the back of The Court. During the 2nd World War the hut was used by a family evacuated from London. When Mrs Carne-Hill died in 1943, she left the hut to the WI with £100 to buy a patch of ground and re-site it. They approached my father who sold them a plot of land for £20 behind the pound and it was re-erected there. We had our 40th anniversary there. I'm not sure when it was pulled down and when we moved to the village hall, but sometime in the early 1960s." Joy Vigar (née Sherrin)

Women's Institute party in Old Hall, late 1940s

"I joined the WI when I was about 14. There wasn't much else for young girls to do then in the village. We had speakers or crafts. We made handbags and lampshades. We used to hold whist drives and whist matches with The British Legion." Joy Vigar (née Sherrin)

"When mum went to WI meetings us children would say, 'Mother's going to the Wild Indians'." Henry Ford

Women's Institute Anniversary cake cutting, 1960

High Ham Women's Institute Recorder Group, 1965

British Legion Dinner in the Women's Institute Old Hall, c1960

"We, the Legion, put on flower shows, big flower shows, a really sizeable flower show, in the hall – and dances, lots of dances." Dennis Davis

"Mrs Carne-Hill and the Reverend Hughes died during the Second World War, within a year of each other, and for a while village life seemed to stop. She had organised so much of it in aid of The Nursing Association - all the plays were done for that. Reverend Hughes had organised fetes and garden parties at the Rectory for the parish in aid of church funds, so there had been a lot going on at the time before the war." Joy Vigar (née Sherrin)

Children's Parties

"To come to the children's Christmas Party the children all had to go to High Ham School, or be born in the village. They were usually in January or, if the weather was bad, then March. There were about 100 children, they'd sit down at tables when they arrived, they learnt to do it properly and they'd have a sandwich - cheese or egg or one of their favourites were pilchards, pilchard sandwiches. Then they had a sausage roll, then cakes, they could only take one at a time. Then they had jelly and trifle. Then we took the tables down and they'd have a couple of games. Maybe musical chairs or passing balloons under the chin and then they'd line up for their ice-cream in cones. They always had to make an orderly line. Then after the ice-cream there were a couple more games like musical buses or the penny tin and then there was the entertainment, a magic show with a conjurer. I paid three guineas for the conjurer in 1964. It was always a proper show. It always finished off with duster hockey - they loved that!" Dulcie Davis

High Ham Christmas Party, early 1950s

"We would have a wonderful tea at the party and an orange in those days - the orange used to come wrapped in tissue paper and some sweets all wrapped up. That was our excitement."
Margaret Porter (née Webb)

"We always used to play hockey at the Christmas parties, it was famous, you had to make these lines of the old wooden chairs and a chair at each end was the goal. We had these sticks which had been cut from wood no doubt, they weren't really hockey sticks but they were a bit resembling them, and they had a rolled up sack bag tied up with a knot, that was a ball and they nominate a number and you had to jump out from each side, grab the stick and charge into it and try and hit it between the chair legs for a goal. All the kids would be sat on each side and get smacked in the head with the sticks, it was good fun, it was fantastic." Brian Hill

Duster Hockey at the children's Christmas Party

High Ham Children's Christmas Party, c1950

Blackberries and Bridgwater Fair

"Where we used to make money was blackberrying. That was our money for Bridgwater Fair. At Northhill, Mrs. Dacey took the blackberries. In the 1920s the most I was paid was tuppence a pound. The best ones went for jam, but the rest were put in a barrel and went for dye. They were a penny a pound." Ron Tapscott

"In the 1930s, Mr. Duddridge used to come with his horse and cart to collect the blackberries from your house. He had the scales on the back of the cart and used to weigh them then and there."
Edna Webb (née Sherrin)

"We always picked blackberries. One day we picked a hundredweight and the wheel buckled on mother's bicycle going home from the weight of them." Rita Vigar (née Ford)

"Another highlight was Bridgwater Fair. You had to go to Bridgwater Fair or you hadn't lived!" Dulcie Davis

"There was a bus trip to Bridgwater Fair after the war. We used to go with Mum and Dad. I got lost and had to stand at the entrance to the big field until somebody came along. They were frantic 'cos they thought they'd lost me." Gwen Chubb (née Bown)

"I used to pick blackberries for the money to go to Bridgwater Fair, otherwise I'd have no money for the rides. I remember walking all down through the road with all the cheapjacks either side. We'd go straight through the fairfield down to the animals, the sheep and the horses. We'd look at them and then Mum and I would have a go on the gallopers." Val Scriven (née Webb)

"In the 1950s they were threepence a pound and went up to sixpence. We took them to Mrs. Shepherd on our bikes to a shed round the back. I remember putting a drop of water in with them so they weighed a bit more! We saved all our money up. If we had five shillings for the fair that was wonderful. The sideshows - you could pay sixpence and see the shortest man and the fattest lady. It were a big outing. We never went shopping, but at Bridgwater Fair, money was spent. We bought towels crockery, cups. That was the biggest market."
Margaret Porter (née Webb)

Bonfire night

"The field hedges were cut and trimmed by hand in the autumn by my father and Uncle Perce - the trimmings were then put into making the annual bonfire (it was an unofficial competition amongst the big farms as to who could make the biggest, brightest bonfire, and on Firework Night you could look all around and see bonfires all over the village, this was in the late 1950s). Our bonfire was usually quite large and my father would light it and then he would light the fireworks and rockets. My mother would cook jacket potatoes in the hot ashes, and sausages... oh happy memories!" Stephen Julian Wheadon

"We always had a bonfire for Guy Fawkes, it was exciting, it was usually at the Webbs, when we were children we used to take a milk churn float around endlessly beforehand, we used to drag it all over the place collecting wood and we used to make a guy - it used to sit in a chair at home and spook us." Gillian Clothier (née Vigar)

Carol singing

"In the winter we had carol singers. We used to load a piano onto a tractor. My uncle would have the piano tuned. By the end of going out for a fortnight it became rather 'sweet'. I played that. We played and sung every night for a fortnight to three weeks. We went all round the parish, Beer, High Ham… it was a long way to go when you were singing for everyone. We sang three verses of a carol, we visited every house and we collected money for the Agricultural Benevolent Fund and some money went towards the harvest festival. People were very generous." Molly Cullen (née Cook)

Low Ham carol singers, 1956. To accompany the singers, a piano was loaded onto a trailer and taken round the village.

Bellringing

*"No bells were rung during the war, it was like a blackout, no noise, no lights. I know that our bells were overhauled in 1919, just after the war. They were rung every Remembrance Day from 1921, they were always muffled for Remembrance Day and funerals. In the past, the vicar would have wanted them rung every Sunday for the service. They'd ring for Club Day, weddings, Royal occasions and other celebrations or events in the village – any excuse! The ringers used to get food and drink for weddings. They didn't ring for money then. Albert 'Hacky' Crossman, he was the Tower Captain, then Simon Spearing took it on, then Arthur Scriven. Jack Cullen, Jo Hurd, Cliff Crossman, Andrew and Fred Ford, Ted Priddle, they were all ringers. There wasn't so much entertainment before the 1950s so ringing was probably the highlight of the week then, a social occasion, they just met every week and rang the bells – they'd have a drink up in the tower and I daresay they'd finish up at the drinking house on the little green or in the pub. Harry Inder wasn't a ringer, but I know he would often appear up the tower with a flagon of his cider. The bellringers had an outing every year, they'd go round the village and ask people to contribute to their outing. I know that Mr Hartley, who lived in the Old School House, would jokingly offer Simon Spearing a sum of money **not** to ring the bells!"* John Vigar, Tower Captain

High Ham belllringers. Photograph taken on Nora Ford's wedding day, 16 June 1951.
Left to right: Benny Hurd, Norman Crossman, Simon Spearing, Ted Priddle, Albert 'Hacky' Crossman, Fred Crossman, Clifford Crossman

"Every Armistice Day when we rang a muffled peal, Hacky Crossman would cry quietly while he was ringing. He'd have his medals in his pocket. We never said anything to him." Graham Scriven

Bellringers' outing to Gough's caves, Cheddar, 1930s

"RIGHT. STAND BY YOUR ROPE. LOOK TO EVERYBODY. TREBLE'S GOING. SHE'S GONE. I've been a ringer at St Andrew's since I was 12 years old. I was taught by my dad Arthur Scriven and Simon Spearing. Going back to the 1930s, Hayman Scriven, my grandfather, Great Uncles Bill and Alb Crossman, all rang at St. Andrew's. Mum can remember seeing them ride their bikes to different towers to ring. In turn, they taught their children, nephews Norman and Cliff Crossman, Andrew and Fred Ford, and my dad. There have been ringers in my family for many years. CLOSE UP AT THE BACK." Maggie Hibberd (née Scriven)

"It was funny because Albert Crossman was the captain of the bellringers up here, and Simon Spearing. John Cook and Robert Parker, Andrew Ford and Fred Ford and Arthur Scriven and Albert Crossman used to sneak up gallons of cider up there, drink a lot of that and put the world straight. They'd smoke Woodbines, and where the clock weights were, they used to fling all their old fag packets. There must be millions down there if they ever clean it. This was in the 1950s." Brian Hill

"My family have all been bellringers. Grandfather and his brother and my brothers all took to it, my two sons and son-in-law. They used to have Christmas parties and we used to go one year to one ringer's home and another year to another ringer's home, and used to hear these songs. You'd say when you met next time, 'Here Tom, let's have that song again, I remember you sang it last time...'"
Amy Ford (née Crossman) [6]

"The Church Council has received from Mr G. Cox his resignation of the office of Captain of the Ringers.
The Council does not accept the resignation of Mr G. Cox, and wishes to retain his services as Captain of the Ringers.
The Council regrets the serious quarrelling has occurred in the Belfry, and decides unanimously that, unless sufficient guarantee is given before Sunday April 27 that no more quarrelling will take place and that the Captain's ruling will always be loyally accepted, it will disband the present Band of Ringers and re-form a Band pledged to loyalty to the Captain.
Meanwhile the present Band of Ringers is requested not to ring the bells.
In order to have the Bells rang on Easter Day the Council has appointed a temporary Band to ring that day."
Letter to The High Ham Church Bellringers from The High Ham Parochial Church Council (date sent unknown)

High Ham Ringers at St. Marys Huish Episcopi, c1960. Back row: Arthur Scriven, Ron Trot, Ralph Cullen; Front row: Graham Cullen, Andrew Ford, John Shire, Albie Lewis, Fred Lewis, Albert 'Hacky' Crossman, Fred Ford, Simon Spearing

The Bells of St Andrew's Church, High Ham
Treble: cast by Robert Austen 2nd of Compton Dundon 1665. Recast by Llwellins and James of Bristol, 1887. Weight 5cwt. 0 qrs. 23lbs. Note B flat.
Second: cast by Robert Austen 1st of Compton Dundon 1641. Weight 6cwt. 3qrs. 8lbs. Note A flat.
Third: cast c1450. Weight: 9cwt. 1qrs. 14lbs. Note G.
Fourth: cast by Thomas Bayley of Bridgwater 1763. Weight 12cwt. 1qrs. 4lbs. Note F.
Tenor: cast by George Davis of Bridgwater 1795. Weight 17cwt. 1qrs. 2lbs. Note E flat old concert pitch.

The Death of the King and the Coronation

"I remember when the King died. Jack Cox, he was our neighbour. He was very deaf, and he couldn't get his radio to work. He came round to us saying his radio was broke and all he could get was this sort of horrible music, and we kept shouting at him, 'The King is dead' and he kept shouting back, 'I can't hear you, what are you saying?' and we were shouting, 'The King's dead, the King's is dead'. It was quite funny."
Rene Winter (née Webb)

Coronation of Queen Elizabeth II at Cook's Farm, Low Ham, 1953. Amy Ford holding the cake

"My uncle had a television. There were only two at that time in Low Ham. He opened up the barn down on the farm and all the people from Low Ham came and watched on this black and white television in the barn. It was amazing. I shall never forget early that morning, my sister and I got in early to church and rang the bells. It was about five in the morning and later we were asked, 'What were you young'uns doing in the church at that time?' But we thought it was a day of celebrations so, here we go! During the day all of the girls turned up with new dresses. Mrs Ford, my parents and other helpers made cakes and we had drinks down there. It was four or five hours and everyone just sat on these planks in the barn watching the television. It was amazing that we were connected with the event we could see for real. It wasn't hearsay or a photograph or a newspaper - we saw it as it was happening."
Molly Cullen (née Cook)

Clock given coat of paint

HIGH Ham displayed great loyalty and jollification on the occasion of the Queen's Coronation. The day opened with a service at the Parish Church and a sports programme was arranged for children and adults. This was followed by a football match between Henley and Low Ham which caused much amusement and was won by Low Ham.

Tea was provided free for all children and old people and each child received a souvenir mug.

In the evening a social gathering was held at the Village Hall.

A television set was provided for public viewing in a barn at Low Ham where light refreshments were served.

To commemorate the Coronation the clock on the church tower was given a new coat of paint.

"Later in the day it went a bit quiet so sports were quickly arranged by Harry Inder, Amy Ford and my father Hubert Hill. There were many races for different age groups like egg and spoon, sack race, three legged race, greasy pole pillow fight and running round Low Ham Church. This became an annual event for many years held in Low Ham Church field." Shirley Badman (née Hill)

Above: Low Ham Sports Day, 1955. Mary Board pulling (front), Annie Skeet (behind). Lads watching: Ron Skeet (left), Andrew Ford (right)

Carnivals and Fetes

High Ham Pageant, c1912. Ada Vigar, 3rd left

High Ham Pageant, 1912. School pupils' 'Nursery Rhymes' entry with teacher, Miss Sherrin

Dressed up for the Rectory Fete, 1920s. Ann Vigar, far right. The two young boys are Gordon Vigar and Vigar Webb

Dennis Davis (aged five) dressed as bookie Bill Kimber for the Rectory Fete, 1934

Maypole dancing, High Ham Rectory garden, 1950. Left to right. Back row: Brenda Martin, Sheila Scriven, Gillian Cook, Olive Brown, Molly Upham, Pamela Osborne, Shirley Hill, Gwen Bown, Jane Upham, Primrose Loader, Sheila Inder. Front row: Greta Loader, Brenda Stone, Ronald Wheadon, Kathleen Bown, Christine Meaker

"We used to have the maypole in the rectory. We made our costumes out of crepe paper." Gwen Chubb (née Bown)

"At one carnival the families from Park went as Park's Circus. They dressed as circus people and rode horses that pranced. Another time they went as ancient Britons. They wore skins, carried large bones and old trees, and coloured their skins with coffee. They also took their floats to Langport Carnival. Other families took part in the High Ham carnivals like the Williams from Henley and the Fords and Scrivens from Low Ham." Joy Vigar (née Sherrin)

Fete/Carnival High Ham, 1940s

High Ham Carnival, 1950. Dulcie and Dennis Davis dressed as Jack and Jill.

1951 Festival of Britain Carnival High Ham

"The carnival entries would parade around the village, finishing off at the Football Field, the field at the junction of Field and Windmill Road. Mum did all the organising and made the costumes for our family's carnival entries. She picked the subject and the people. Mum was good at sewing, she used a treadle machine, sewing and singing." Henry Ford

Amy Ford's entry 'Britannia and the Commonwealth' awarded 2nd prize, 1951. Bob Scriven (Scotland), Arthur Scriven (New Zealand), Amy Ford (Britannia), behind Amy, Joe Fisher, Fred Ford (Australia), Alma Ford (South Africa), Phyllis Scriven (Wales), Vera Scriven (Ireland), Rita Ford (Canada)

Photograph taken day of the High Ham Fete in aid of the Village Hall funds. The Village Hall committee. Left to right: Mr P Clarke (secretary), Mr G A Baucham (chairman), Mr H Bellot (owner), Mrs B Hartley, Mr E Priddle (caretaker)

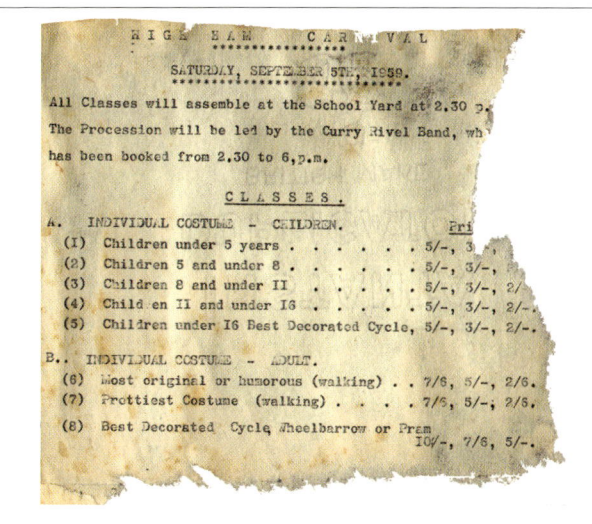

Fragment of High Ham Carnival classes leaflet, 5 September 1959

Chapel and Church Festivals

Harvest Festival at Low Ham Chapel, 1900-1910 [7]

"We had anniversaries. We had to learn a piece and say it in front of everybody. We were in a new frock. We used to have two new frocks a year, one for Easter and one for Anniversary. Tom (Oram) used to set us little things. Once we had to look for the shortest verse in the Bible. We used to read something and sing choruses. It was a lovely tea and then we had games, 'Here we coming gathering nuts in May', Tug of War... When we came out we had an orange, a bun and a shilling. That was why we went to Sunday School because of the Christmas parties and the outings." Margaret Porter (née Webb) (Henley Chapel)

"Every year we would have an anniversary. We had to learn our recitations. Now I know where they came from - it was the hymn books - so I know a lot of the hymns off by heart now."
Molly Cullen (née Cook) (Low Ham Chapel)

Henley Chapel Sunday School, 1950s

"Rector Crossman used a four-wheel coach, he used to visit people, but he didn't visit the Chapel people and that remained until Rector Hughes arrived. That was about 1926/7. Rector Hughes visited everybody in the parish. John Oram, the Chapel man, said that Reverend Hughes was a very nice man. Chapel and Church were two separate religions. Crossman was a wealthy man, you had to lift your hat. Rector Hughes changed things. On Armistice Sunday the British Legion used to have a parade, they walked up to the pub after the service, and Rector Hughes walked with them and had a drink with them." Ron Tapscott

"I remember one year someone brought a donkey into the Church at High Ham during the service on Palm Sunday for a joke. There was a lot of confusion as they tried to get rid of it outside. That was when Mrs Carne-Hill was alive." Dennis Davis

Rogation Sunday at Low Ham, 1950s

"Rogation Sunday was a big feast at Low Ham. People paraded around, you were supposed to walk the boundaries, in fact you didn't, but you walked a long way, and faced North, South, East and West and the crops and animals were blessed. It was a bit similar to wassailing. I recall fund raising activities and parties, Low Ham used to rise to the occasion at Easter, Rogation, Christmas and especially Harvest. They would bring extra seats in, and it was amazing where people came from. Why to Low Ham? Whether it was in the middle of a farmyard field and it was different? Everyone togged up in their best, the ladies wore hats. On Palm Sunday Paul Thomas would organise a donkey. It stayed outside the church and then it would go with the congregation for the procession outside." Molly Cullen (née Cook)

"The Reverend Downing was a wonderful man. He was vicar at High Ham in the late 1950s. He ran a very good Sunday School and once he took the children down to Paradise, because he thought it was appropriate. Coming back he wasn't concentrating where he was going and went into a ditch. He came to our door saying, 'I ditched my vehicle' and to ask to be towed out. Henry said, 'Well it's milking time, it will just have to stay there'. Later in the evening he went down and pulled him out." Joy Vigar (née Sherrin)

"One of the best days was Ascension Day. We had to go to school and then we all went to church in the morning. We took flowers, bluebells, peonies, daffodils, cowslips, cow parsley to place in a huge crown with vases which was raised in pride of place on the rood screen in the Church. We always sang 'Jesus Christ is risen today' and 'There is a Green Hill Far Away'. The leavers were given a special treat of going up the tower and looking out. Then we had half day off."
Gillian Clothier (née Vigar)

Ascension Day Parade, 27 May 1965

Other Village Pastimes

Mrs Carne-Hill's drama group, Guy Tapscott far left

"It was the Somerset Annual Drama Competition, we were always beaten by a boys' club from the Poldens. I remember I just had to come in wheeling this thing around and shouting 'Tarts!'." Guy Tapscott

"In the 1930s Mrs Carne-Hill used to have us up at the Court when we were young, we used to practice these plays and then we went and did them at other places. We went to Edington. We had to make sound effects. We had two coconuts to hit together to make the sound of horses' hooves and we wound a ribbon round and round which made the sound of the wind and when we'd done our practice Mrs Carne-Hill would say, 'I'll make tea and get Louise to bring in the rock cakes', and I remember Guy saying once that he ate nine rock cakes!"
Ethel Webb

1922 The 'Annual Challenge Cup' was awarded to Hayman Scriven, Gares Cottage, Low Ham for 'A well-kept garden in High Ham'. The cup was given by Sir Ernest Jardine of Nottingham, a local Somerset MP.

"We used to have a keep fit class in the hall. It was run by Mrs Woods, the butcher's wife in Langport. She used to have music on a radio. It was great fun. There were about 30 of us. We used to do it in the village hall once a week then we used to go round doing demonstrations at village fetes, Aller, Langport, Long Sutton, we enjoyed it, entertaining people at fetes. I don't know that we were that good." Dulcie Davis

The Keep Fit Group, c1960

"We used to cycle to dances in Moorlinch and Aller. We'd come back in the dark up Turn Hill. My dad was dead against us putting on lipstick so we'd go behind the chapel and put it on. Oh yes we had a lot of fun."
Gwen Chubb (née Bown)

"In the 1940s, 50s and 60s in this village there was a men's Conservative club, ladies' Conservative club and a young Conservatives club. They were all going strong and after the war Father ran a successful youth club. There were youth club dances, Conservative dances and a football team. There was a band played for the dances, a bloke from Glastonbury came and Ernie Elkins and Ken Duddridge used to play concertinas. It was a very lively village and thriving pub. There was a pantomime and there used to be a village party for the children every year. It was started by the British Legion but then I took it over and ran it for 40 years and the British Legion and the WI used to run whist drives. There could be 40 tables for whist drives sometimes. The British Legion and Young Farmers would combine forces to put one on. There were tables everywhere. I remember winning a live goose once. I carried it home under my arm. I was so proud I put it in the coal shed for the night, but my husband thought I'd want it as a pet so he got his father to kill it before morning!" Dulcie Davis

Life at School

From the Beginning

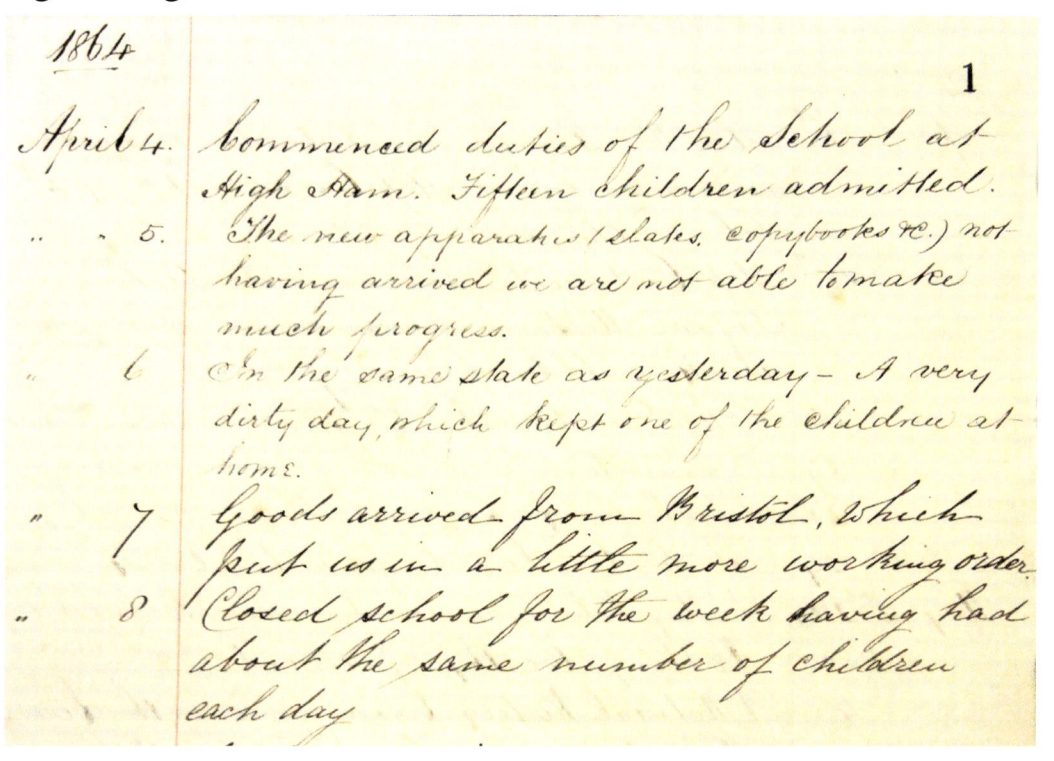

> 1864
> April 4. Commenced duties of the School at High Ham. Fifteen children admitted.
> " 5. The new apparatus (slates, copybooks &c.) not having arrived we are not able to make much progress.
> " 6 In the same state as yesterday – A very dirty day which kept one of the children at home.
> " 7 Goods arrived from Bristol, which put us in a little more working order.
> " 8 Closed school for the week having had about the same number of children each day

18 June 1897: Women's Benefit Society's Anniversary School closed on Thursday and Friday of this week also on June 21st, 22nd, 23rd on the occasion and in commemoration of Queen Victoria's Diamond Jubilee. The school children had a tea in the playground which was covered. [1]

1 July 1898: For the last two weeks haymaking has taken a large number of boys in the upper-class, several are also away picking peas. [1]

> "The average attendance continues low, and there was rather a large number absent from the Examination.
> G. Eden Peake, Diocesan Inspector."

1898 Extract from High Ham School Log Book [1]

High Ham School, late 1890s
Headteacher Mr Mathams with his wife and pupils

Getting to School

"I started school in 1923 when I was 4. We used to wear these muffs, put your hands in to go to school with sometimes a baked apple too, a hot one, you always had a hot oven, we used to put an apple in and put it in our muff, it would be nice and warm then and we ate it."
Linda Lavis (née Gould)

"We walked up to school on our own, all together, a number of us, no adults. The first year you had someone to look after you, one of the older ones, but after the first year you never bothered, you found your way up and found your way home."
Ron Tapscott

"Well, I started up Ham School when I was four years old walking up from down Henley. I can remember coming up to school and Stembridge Hill was covered with stones, it was just a track and I remember ice being on the ground and trying to crawl up over the hill to get to school. I remember that as if it were yesterday, that was the 1920s."
Frances Webb (née Weech)

"In the 1920s and 30s when you got to about seven or eight you always had jobs to do when you got home. One thing which practically all the children in the countryside had to do was find some 'morning sticks', small sticks to light the fire. That was an important job. We'd do it on the way home from school. There were always some around. There was a boy up the road, he was always shouting out, 'Oh, I haven't got my morning sticks, come on, help me with my morning sticks'. We were always playing on the way to school. Even if it was raining nobody came to fetch us and if you never had a mac you got wet."
Ron and Guy Tapscott

"I didn't have to do anything before I went to school just a few odd things. But I remember I used to have to let the fowls out. When they used to grow corn they used to move the hens out on the stubble and let the hens pick up the corn that was left. I had to go and let them out before I went to school and we had a cob horse that we used to ride."
Ethel Webb

"There was the Vigars and the Groves family who lived opposite at Park Farm Dairy. Uncle Joe, my mother's brother, he had four daughters and a son. They all walked to Ham school, Henry and his sister Peggy, and the Weeches, they used to walk out to Moreton Corner, and the ones from Park, and whoever got there first in the morning always put a stone out to say they had gone on. We always had a school bell that used to ring at quarter to nine and Henry used to say that if they were at the top of Stembridge and the bell went, they had to hurry."
Joy Vigar (née Sherrin)

"Occasionally we would get a lift to school in the summer with Mr Coombes who had a field below us where he came for milking twice a day. He had a car with a pull down roof and stood the churns in the back. We would be just leaving the garden gate when he came on - lucky! Others from the other end of the village could get a ride up to school with the postman - if the right one was on duty that morning."
Guy Tapscott

"In the 1940s we used to walk to High Ham School. In the afternoon the big red mail van used to be coming along at going home time and he very often gave us a lift. There were quite a gang of us."
Gwen Chubb (née Bown)

The Village School

1930s postcard of the Infant, Junior and Senior Schools, High Ham [2]

"I was five when I went to school in 1934. There was a Headmistress, her name was Miss Smith, an eccentric sort of person. She lived in the School House, which was next door to the school, it was the old school and joining that was the Headmaster's house, that's all gone now. And there were two other teachers, Miss Sherrin, who lived in the house opposite the school where Miss Warne lived, and I can't remember the infant teacher's name. There were three classes: the Infants, where you started at five, then you moved up to Miss Sherrin in the middle, then Miss Smith when you were about nine. I voluntarily left when I was 11 because I was dead keen to go to Huish School. There were two or three other lads in the village who went too, the others stayed there in High Ham till 14. I stayed in Huish till I was 14 and started working." Dennis Davis

The 1900s to 1920s

Headteacher Mr Mathams, High Ham School, 1904 [3]

Miss Emily Sherrin with her class, High Ham School, 1913

April 29th 1910
The Annual Prize Distribution and Entertainment in the schoolroom, the registers not marked in the afternoon, the master away from 10a.m. until afternoon school on Monday as it was necessary to procure a license for the entertainment.[1]

May 27th 1910
School closed on account of Men's Friendly Society. Dinner in schoolroom. This festival is generally held during the Whitsun holiday, but owing to the death of His Majesty The King, it was postponed to this date.[1]

Extract taken from High Ham School Log Book [1]

"I was born in 1912 and I remember Mr Mathams. He taught me. He had been at the school since he was young. He retired when he was about 70, when I was 10 or 11. He taught everyone in the village and everybody loved him.
I loved school. I loved learning and that's why I persuaded mother to let me stay on for an extra year. I stayed until I was 15. Mr. Bennett was the headteacher then. I was the only one in my year, so they just let me read books for that extra year. I loved it."
Freda Hayes (née Cullen)

8 August 1919
Peace Celebration in connection with a fete in the grounds of Ham Court. Bank Holiday excursion of Congregational Sunday Schools of Low Ham and Henley. School dismissed until 15th September, one week extra vacation being given for the Blessings of Victory and Peace.[1]

Bulb and Flower Show

High Ham School Bulb Show prize winners, 1912

Bulb growing competition under Mr Jardine's scheme started for the 3rd successive year. The entries close the 1st week in October.

26 Gave notice as to the Bulb competition to commence the 1st week in October
Oct 3rd In the bulb growing, 136 competitors entered in 8 classes, with 243 bulbs.
Class 1. 48 com 48 bulbs | Class 5. 9 com 27 bulbs
    2. 13 - 39 | 6. 14 - 14
    3. 15 - 15 | 7. 9   - 27
    4. 13 - 13 | 8. 15 - 60

The competition among the children in the collection of wild flowers, pressed and named, was very keen. a large number entered
Bunches of wild flowers proved attractive. The judge of wild flowers was J. H. Burton Esqre County instructor in agriculture.

1912 Extracts taken from High Ham School Log Book [1]

The 1920s

"We used to stay in one class, we never moved out, only when we were told to. Three classes. We didn't have a heater in each class, just one in the whole school, in the middle of two classes. They had another little one for when the nurse did come, for your teeth. We used to have our teeth done there, see if your chest was alright, examine 'ee and check for nits. Your parents put paraffin on your head to get rid of them. And we never went to any doctors, it were all done at school. Like when the dentist come to see to your teeth. Your parents didn't come, they didn't have time. My mother never came and saw me have my teeth out."
Linda Lavis (née Gould)

"Singing was one lesson held at school, for this my father and another boy used to be sent out of the class until it was over, they of course had a great time playing, 'unsupervised', in an empty classroom until it was time to return. Singing was not one of my father's talents and he much preferred the arrangement."
Paula Fisher (née Lloyd)

"Oh, the cane, from the Headmaster - it was normally a hazel. We had a combustion stove for a fire, one in each room and of course we used to heat the poker and put it down through the boards, and there was always a hole down there in the floorboards, and the cane would always go down there, one of the boys would put it down, always the boy who got the cane most, sometimes it was too long to go down then it had to be bent, pushed in there, there was no way of getting it out! We didn't see any danger, I suppose the danger would have been if it had burnt down the school - oh, if it had burnt down the school, well that would have been alright!"
Ron Tapscott

"The cane was with the headmaster, he had it on his desk. He was at the end, he used to be up there high on his desk. 'Up on the carpet' they used to say. That meant you had to go up. Some of them used to put a hair on their hand, you don't feel it so bad so they said. You had to put your hand out, and your hand would come back sometimes, then you'd get it harder next time. They used to do naughty things then. They used to go blackberrying in their dinner hour and then they might be late getting back, well it wasn't dinner, it was only a sandwich we took with us, we used to sit round the stove, the big stove, and then somebody would have a toasting fork and try to toast their sandwich. It was a big high stove, that's all the heat we had."
Linda Lavis (née Gould)

"I don't forget the schoolmaster… I were left handed and he would walk down by me and put the ruler across my hand 'cos I was left handed to make me use my other hand. Soon as he went on I had to put it back again as I couldn't write at all with my other. Well, as a matter of fact we shouldn't be wicked I know, but he broke his leg and we kids were as pleased as punch!"
Frances Webb (née Weech)

"The infant teacher I had when I started was Miss Eavis and she used to ride a racer bike and leave it in Miss Sherrin's house. Marshall Hill at Low Ham, when I was coming on to starting school, he said to me, 'You'll be up with Miss Legs next week'. Course, I went up and called her Miss Legs, didn't I – thought that were her name, see."
Frances Webb (née Weech)

High Ham School, c1928. Headmaster Mr Bennett
Left to right. Back row: Reg Davey, Charles Shepherd, Sydney Male, Joe Lambert, Cyril Lloyd. 3rd row: Grace Gould, Flo Cox, Rosaline Cox, Edith Richards, Marjory Hill, Jenny Hoare. 2nd row: George Richards, Victor Richards, Phyllis Groves, Den Cox, Harry Inder, Leonard Lloyd. Front row includes Harold Lavis, Wilson Cox, Ken Cox

6 July 1920
A pouring wet morning very few children (Infants 7) attended, some had to return home wet through.[1]

18 January 1926
Six inches of snow. Mrs Carne-Hill asked to be allowed to speak a few words to the children on feeding the birds while the snow is on the ground.[1]

7 June 1928
Small attendance owing to WI outing to Torquay.[1]

The 1930s

High Ham Primary School, 1935. Teacher Mrs Ablett
Left to right. Back row: Freda Brooks, Lucy Oram, Joan Skeet, ?, Clifford Webb, Nellie Tapscott, Edna Sherrin, Gertie Knapp. Front row: Ted Brooks, Ted Hollard, Joy Sherrin, Irene Jenkins, Maria Dolly, Stella Bartlett, John Wheadon, Roy Jenkins, Dennis Davis

The Snow Queen Production, 1937. Miss Smith, headmistress, and Miss Sherrin, deputy.
"I was the Snow Queen aged 7 at High Ham School."
Diana Dunthorn (née Bassett)

High Ham School, 1935

1910 - 1935
Silver Jubilee Year of their Majesties, the King & Queen.

6 May 1935
School closed for King's Silver Jubilee. A gramophone, HMV Table model, 3 dozen records bought for school use.[1]

"Mrs Knowles and Miss Smith were the teachers when I was there in the 30s, Miss Smith used to tuck her skirts into her large bloomers when she took us for PT." Dennis Davis

High Ham School, 1936

18 November 1935
Sandford, charabanc proprietor of Langport, was interviewed. After provisionary arrangements had been negotiated with him, the head saw the parents requesting their permission to the children being conveyed by bus. As an experiment this was done this Monday morning … on wet mornings children from Low Ham, Henley and Bere are conveyed by charabanc. The parents defraying the cost of 3d per head.[1]

28 January 1936
Funeral of His Majesty King George V. Children assembled at 10.30am. Union Jack flown. March to church for memorial service. Broadcast of funeral of His Majesty. Listened to by scholars, staff, rector and some parents and others. Union Jack struck 2.40pm. School dismissed.[1]

30 January 1936
School special children's broadcast on the proclamation of King Edward VIII.[1]

Evacuees

The ordinary school routines suffered from continual changes. There are already evacuees in the school, and the children already have gas masks. In early November 'the entire staff' attended the Anti-Gas Lectures for teachers at Langport School. December 11th Mr Goodfellow removed his evacuee grand-daughter from the school, upon her having been bitten for the second time by Bassett's dog.[4]

High Ham School, 1939
Headteacher, Miss Smith (holding the cat) and Miss Louie Sherrin (second row from back, far right)

"I soon settled down to country life, attending High Ham village school. I used to walk there every day with my friends, Alma, Vera and Rita from next door. The seniors (11-14 years) were taught by the headmistress, a very stern woman with short cropped hair and she always seemed to wear the same green tweed suit. She was very fond of using the cane, especially on the boys! I was in Miss Sherrin's class, an outstanding teacher. I am told she never left the school, but went from pupil to teacher. This wouldn't be allowed today. She not only taught the usual subjects, but also sewing, embroidery and knitting. She also had a great gift for reading stories and would always read us part of a story before going home each evening. There were about 30 of us evacuees, we must have doubled the size of the school." Alma Vinter (née Willoughby)

School dinners were begun on 23rd February 1940, served by the Langport Cooking Depot. 64 partaking, 77 on role.

1940 2nd August: In accordance with the LEA's circular letter, the head offered herself to the Women's Land Army for the holidays. She was posted to Aller Dairies as an assistant cheese maker. She did 31 days, Saturday 3rd August 7:30am till Monday 2nd September 7:00pm.

1941 27th February: School closed all day for the erection of the BLACKOUT fixtures.

1944 13th June: This afternoon, as the children are acting two plays for the Salute the Soldier social this evening, a rehearsal was held in the Village Hall from 3:30pm.

1944 16th October: There are 55 local children and 22 evacuees on the roll.

1944 26th November: The first parcels of requisitions have arrived. The goods are rationed and much of what was ordered was unobtainable.

1945 8th and 9th May: These two days are public holidays owing to the cessation of hostilities in Europe.

1945 4th June: The county P.E. Organiser suggested that the railings between the boys' and the girls' playgrounds be removed.

1945 5th September: Today the school reopened after the summer holidays, together with an additional two days for VJ Day.

1945 5th November: Have received seven forms for supplementary clothing coupons for children with feet measuring eight and a half for girls and nine and a half for boys or over.

Extracts taken from High Ham School Log Book [1]

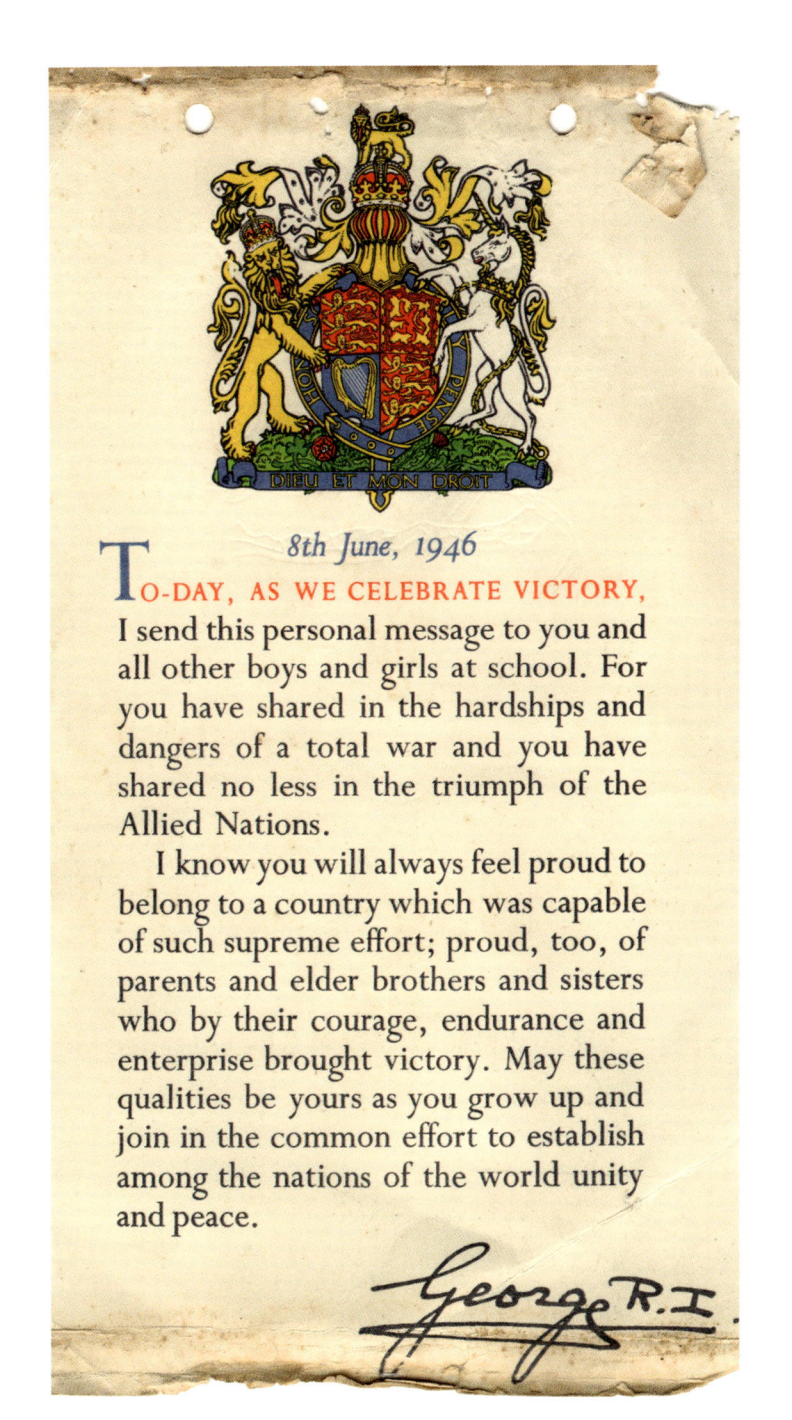

8th June, 1946

TO-DAY, AS WE CELEBRATE VICTORY, I send this personal message to you and all other boys and girls at school. For you have shared in the hardships and dangers of a total war and you have shared no less in the triumph of the Allied Nations.

I know you will always feel proud to belong to a country which was capable of such supreme effort; proud, too, of parents and elder brothers and sisters who by their courage, endurance and enterprise brought victory. May these qualities be yours as you grow up and join in the common effort to establish among the nations of the world unity and peace.

George R.I.

After the War

Miss Louie Sherrin, 19 July 1956. She taught at High Ham School and lived with her sister Emily at The Lodge. They were Ned Sherrin's aunts.

"We had Miss Everitt, she was the first teacher I recall. She was very strict and if you were naughty she would either tie you to a chair or you had to go behind the blackboard. There was always a lot of mischief going on, we liked her though. With Miss Rabbage, we had to stand out in the front and read a page a day, and I was absolutely terrified and I was never ever any good whatsoever, though I read a lot at home. We had PT in the mornings, the girls had to take off their long skirts and put shorts on. We were divided into four groups and we did bunny hops and stretching and so on. We had a couple of sports days. All the schools in the area went to Huish for Sports Day, we trained in the field across the road, and you've never seen such a silly lot of kids, we just ran wild, because it wasn't a playing field, it was an orchard. I won a third once in the obstacle race, it was the first rosette High Ham ever won." Molly Cullen (née Cook)

"Mum came with me when I started school on the first day in 1940s. I think I cried. I didn't like it at all. It was Miss Everitt and Mrs Wilkins and Miss Sherrin came to help out. The two Sherrin sisters were living in The Lodge. Louie, that was her name, used to come across and help. She was one of my teachers. Every week I'd go round the corner to Mr Hunt's, the Post Office, and I would get the Family Allowance. I'd come back into school with it in my purse." Gwen Chubb (née Bown)

"In 1951 I was 14 and I was out on the moor haymaking and the Attendance Officer came out. How he found us I don't know! He found me working with Father and my grandfather. I was up making the rick. The Attendance Officer said to my father, "Your son should be at school." My father said, "Well, if you can find someone to go up there and do what my son's doing, then he can go to school, otherwise he's here for three days!" Len Cox

"When I went in the 1950s the school at the time was also the library for High Ham. They had a big sign outside and it was actually the library for the village, and occasionally they had to calculate how many books were missing, and they used to get all us kids involved, they'd give us a great pile each and we'd have to sit there with our books and they'd shout out whatever they were looking for, and we'd have to say 'Yeah, got it!'.
Mrs Ivy Cullen used to be the dinner lady, and do the odd jobs, keep the fire going - two great coal fires in the school. There used to be a school kitchen roughly where Tesco is now in Langport. A lot of people worked in this place, they would cook all the food there, and vans would bring it out to the outlying areas, in these big aluminum tins. Most people had school dinners.
In the early days the travelling gypsies would appear and Ham school took them, one day there were 30 of us in the school and the next day, there were 50. And some of the gypsy kids had never been to school at all. So you'd get allocated one and a half gypsy children to look out for. They used to borrow furniture from the village hall. The gypsy kids all lived down at Harry Inder's." Brian Hill

"The teachers when I went to school were Miss Everitt and Miss Rabbage. I was in Miss Rabbage's class and one day I thought I've had enough of this so I asked to go to the toilet. I went out and jumped over the wall. It was only about two foot high back then. I started walking home and met Mum coming down the road, she was going to work. She caught me, gave me a clip round the ear and took me back to school. It only took one clip round the ear as I never bunked off again. They put up a wire fence after that." Gary Mitchell

---

24 June 1950: Today as a perfect attendance had been made throughout the week, a half an hour extra play was given. [1]

Playtime

"We played games in the playground. The girls played 'buttons' and skipping, 'buttons' in the spring, skipping in the summer. It was governed by the weather. We didn't play with hoops, the boys played with hoops, they didn't play 'buttons'. For 'buttons' we got our mothers to give us some of their buttons from their button jar and we drew six squares in the dust or the mud. You threw your button into the first square, then had to hop and pick it up, then hop round the other squares. Then you threw your button into square number two and so on. If you didn't get your button in the square or hopped on any lines you were out and it was the next person's turn." Freda Hayes (nee Cullen)

"I had a whip and a top and used to send it whirling down the road. I had roller skates. It was all done in the road. We had marbles and played conkers. I used to cook them in the bottom oven to make them stronger. There was one game that was quite good. It was called Tin Can Kettle. There would be several of us and you'd be out in the yard to play this. A tin can was put in the middle of the yard. Someone would be the killer, while the rest of us hid. The killer, if they saw someone, would call out their name at the same time as touching the can. That person was out and had to stand near the tin can. Once there were two or three of you standing by the can, if one of you could kick the can before the killer saw you, then all of you were back in the game again. We used to play that for ages. None of our games cost anything. We used to come out of school at playtime to do skipping on The Green. We'd take it in turns turning the skipping rope and used to just run in and out doing skipping games, all of us jumping in together up and down. There was no traffic. We were quite safe." Joy Vigar (nee Sherrin)

"We were always playing in the road. We played five stones and hopscotch. Oh and skipping. We all had skipping ropes. You'd start off with just one skipping, then another would jump in with you. We'd have a rope across the road with someone turning each end. Then one would run in and jump up and down then another then another as many as was playing. One rhyme I remember was 'One potato (one person would run in and jump), two potato, three potato, four and out' and you would have to come out. Another thing was to make the rope go round twice before you landed, even three times if you were good. If there was a lot of us we would play 'The Farmer's in his Den'. We'd play that at school in a big circle. Another game was 'Lucy Locket'. 'Piggy in the Middle' was another good game. We were all good at playing with balls. We could juggle them against the wall of the house, two or three balls at a time. We would sort of leapfrog over the ball or make it bounce singing these rhymes. If you dropped a ball you were out. Handstands were another thing we did against the side of the house. You would do a handstand and then walk down the wall till your feet were touching the ground and then try and walk around, a big upside down 'u'. We'd collect car numbers, see how many we could get before we had to go in for tea. One would collect black car numbers, another red ones, make a game of it." Gwen Chubb (nee Bown)

"We used to play rounders a lot in Henry Vigar's field opposite where the bonfires were held. There was Jim Upham, the Pullens and me. We had catapults and used to aim at tin cans on posts. We fired bows and arrows at each other as well, it was a wonder we didn't put an eye out. We did one thing which was quite dangerous looking back on it. We were in Eastfield, the conservation field. Back then Cecil Williams used to milk his cows there. We climbed into the sheep rack that was always there, we just lifted the lid and got in. We pushed it off with a big stick and we went down over the steep hill. We got up a good speed by the time we reached the bottom. I remember it was quite bumpy! We did that quite a few times."
Gary Mitchell

"We used to go rhyne jumping. One of us was always guaranteed to fall in the stinking water up to your neck. But most of the time we were helping out at home or messing about, we didn't play proper games." Graham Scriven

The School Privy

> Received also copy of H.M. Inspector's Report made after visit of 22nd Decr 1904, as under:
> "The boys' porch, used for their cloaks, is not ventilated, and their playground is not in good condition.
> There is no urinal for the Infant boys
> Apex ventilation is needed in the Infant Room.
> Both rooms need painting, cleaning &c, and there are no suitable lavatory arrangements."

Extract taken from High Ham School Log Book [1]

"When I went to school first they were open closets, a plank with a hole, you went in on your own, part of the roof was exposed, you could see the sky. I think toilet paper was just cut up squares of newspaper. Hacky Crossman would come with a tipping putt and a horse and dig out the pit and empty it, probably on the communal allotments, which were where that little field is opposite the Rectory. Oh, they were lovely carrots they grew there!" Peggy Coombes (née Vigar)

"We had our drinking water, it was supplied in a bucket in the playground. We used to drink from that, but the dog used to drink from it, and make use of it, both ends! We used to go up to the village pump too, that was on The Green. Nobody took any notice. If the bucket was empty it was empty. I was there when the new toilets were built, but before that it was the bucket - bucket and chuck-it! After that somebody come round, horse and cart used to come in and put in sawdust and take it out, that was up-to-date that was! We just had a bucket. I don't remember if there was a door there, I don't think there was. This was going back to the 1920s and 30s." Ron and Guy Tapscott

"The boys' toilets were like a urinal, but it was filled with peat, and the famous Hacky, he used to come up and maintain that, and change all this peat around." Brian Hill

"My one unfailing memory of the school (I know this sounds awful) were the wonderful toilets!! A bucket under a wooden bench type seat – open at the back – I now realise for easy emptying. The older boys would get their bicycles pumps and squirt air into the back of the girls' loo. How we hated them!" Irene Stimpson (née Figg)

---

7 November 1949: The 'head nurse' examined all the children's heads today. The school is pronounced 'clean'. [1]

The Big School[5]

"I left school in 1933, I was 13, I went on to work for Father. I was going to Langport Grammar School and it closed through lack of numbers. I could have gone to Taunton or Street, but I had no intention of going there. I persuaded Mother. It was before I was 14 so Mother had to see the Rector and he said 'I'll see to that'."
Ron Tapscott

"I cycled to school every day, to Huish, there was half a dozen of us at least. That was a mixed secondary modern. Not many of the girls went when I went, not till they had to later on. It was opened in 1940, but I don't think there were any girls from High Ham, that I can remember. There were half girls at the school. Langport Grammar School had closed at that time, that was where the dentist surgery was, up Langport Hill. Girls went to Taunton, or Bridgwater to the grammar school. Some of the girls went to the Convent in Langport. The Convent took a lot of girls from High Ham."
Dennis Davis

"The war started the day I started school at Bridgwater when I was 11 and it finished when I finished school at 16. I used to ride my bicycle up to top of Turn Hill and put it in Peppard's shed. Then I walked down the hill, round the hair-pin bend out to the main road. I got on the Langport to Bridgwater bus... Luckily, during the war, the clocks were on double summer time and summer time through the winter, so I used to get home at about half past five and it was just about getting dark, but in the morning I went out in the dark. We used to wear black lisle stockings. The mothers got that changed during the war to white ankle socks, as they couldn't get the coupons for them."
Joy Vigar (née Sherrin)

"I used to have to cycle to Huish School. I always left my bike up Wearne Hollow... and I can guarantee it would be there when I got back. You used to have to cycle to school, but then a bit later they put on a bus. We used to do cookery at school, at Huish that is. Mrs Pitman used to teach us. She lived in High Ham. When you were older we used to have something we called 'A week in the flat'. We were let off all our other subjects and we would spend a week in the flat. We had to clean and cook a meal and invite the teachers for it. That week we would have to do some cooking that we had been taught... clean the flat, wash the bed linen, there was a bed there, then how to iron it all and remake the bed. We had to go and buy all our ingredients to cook the meal. We had a set amount of money. There were two of you doing this. I was in the flat with Shirley Gould from Pitney."
Gwen Chubb (née Bown)

"Huish School was opened just before World War Two. If you could get to the school, you could go there. There was no transport from High Ham. Those from Somerton and Long Sutton could go by train. After the war there was a school bus. It went from The Green. I remember Sheila Hubble was on the first bus. Roy and Guy used to cycle up from Henley and leave their bikes in the Manor."
Joy Vigar (née Sherrin)

"I was at Millfield School, Street and in the winter of 1962-63 they insisted that everyone came to school, whether you were a day pupil or a boarder. There were boarding houses all round here, at Shapwick, Ashcott and High Ham. I walked with the people from High Ham, it took an hour and a quarter with no hanging around, some nights even on Saturdays we didn't get back until about half past seven. That went on for three months. I did manage to cadge a lift one Saturday with the postman, who said, 'Get in my van but don't let anyone see you', I would have been in trouble if seen."
Molly Cullen (née Cook)

"Grace, my younger sister, she was bright, but she failed her 11+ through stammering. You could try again when you were 13, the 13+, but she still failed it the second time because of her stammering. I suppose that wouldn't happen today."
Margaret Porter (née Webb)

HIGH HAM, LOW HAM, ALLER, HENLEY, PITNEY & WEARNE, AGRICULTURAL ASSOCIATION.

PRESIDENT:
Major G. F. Davies, M.P.

THE 70th ANNUAL

PLOUGHING MATCH

will take place on

FRIDAY, OCTOBER 26TH, 1928

On LANDS in the occupation of Mr. J. Cook, Low Ham Farm.

The following Prizes will be Offered for Competition:

CLASS 1.
To the Ploughman who shall Plough best, in a given time, about Half-an-Acre of Land, according to the Rules laid down at the time of drawing Tickets. A SPECIAL OPEN CLASS, open to all comers, 1st Prize £4, 2nd £2, 3rd £1. Third Prize will be withheld if not 5 entries.

CLASS 2.
For the Unmarried Sons of Farmers not having won the Watch in previous years.
1st PRIZE, a handsome SILVER WATCH, given by Miss Reynolds, the driver 2s 6d, 2nd Prize piece of Machinery valued £2 2s, given by Messrs. Hawkes & Sons, Ltd., Taunton, 3rd Prize £1 1s, driver 2s 6d, 4th Prize 10s 6d, driver 2s 6d. Five to compete or the 4th prize will not be awarded. Entrance, 5s each team.

CLASS 3.
1st. Prize, £3 3s., the driver 2s. 6d. 2nd Prize £2 2s., 3rd Prize £1 10s., given by Messrs. Hill & Sawtell, driver 2s. 6d. To be Ploughed for by Farmers and Farmer's Sons having won the 1st Prize in Class 1. Five to compete or the 3rd Prize will not be awarded. Entrance 5s each team.

CLASS 4. Champion Class.
To the Ploughman that has won the 1st or 2nd in any Ploughing Match and residing in the limits of the Association. 1st Prize £2 10s, driver 2s 6d, 2nd Prize £1 10s, driver 2s 6d, 3rd Prize 12s 6d, driver 2s 6d.

CLASS 5.
For Men who have been in regular employment of their Masters as Ploughmen for at least two months.

	£ s. d.		s. d.				s. d.
1st Prize	2 5 0	Given by G. A. L. Skerry, Esq. Driver	5 0	5th Prize	15 0	Given by the Association. Driver	2 6
2nd ditto	1 15 0	" the Association. "	2 6	6th ditto	10 0	" " "	2 6
3rd ditto	1 5 0	" " "	2 6	7th ditto	7 6	" " "	2 6
4th ditto	1 0 0	" " "	2 6				

A Pair of Sheets given by Mr. Maxwell for the best Bye. All unsuccessful competitors in this class will receive 5s.

CLASS 6.
For Boys under 21 years of age who are in the employment of Subscribers of this Association.
1st Prize - 2 0 0 Given by the Association Driver 2 6   3rd Prize - A Pair of Leggings given by Mr. W. Priddle. Driver 2 6
2nd ditto - 1 0 0 " " " 2 6   4th ditto - 7 6 Given by the Association " 2 6
10/6 given by Mr. C. Shire, of Langport, for the Best Bye-Furrow in this Class. Extra Prizes will be given if entries sufficient. No Match Plough or Press Wheel to be used in this Class.

CLASS 7.
Open to Classes 4, 5 and 6. SPECIAL PRIZES will be given for the Cleanest and the Best turned out Team, 1st Prize 15s, 2nd 10s.

CLASS 8.
To the man under 25 years of age who shall best Cut and Lay the Hedge and Dig the Ditch within a given time. 1st Prize £1, 2nd Prize 15s, 3rd Prize 10s, 4th Prize 5s. First and Second Prizewinners for the last three years will not be eligible to compete in Classes 8 and 9.

CLASS 9.
To the man of 25 years of age who shall best Cut and Lay the Hedge and Dig the Ditch within a given time. 1st Prize £1, 2nd Prize 15s, 3rd Prize 10s. Extra prizes will be given if over 5 entries.
A SPECIAL Prize of 10s in each Class will be given by Mr. T. A. Sherrin for the piece of hedge that made the best growth in 1927 Hedging Competition.

CLASS 10.
Special Prize for First and Second winners in Classes 8 and 9 for the last 3 years. 1st Prize £1 5s, 2nd Prize 17s 6d, 3rd Prize 12s 6d.

CLASS 11.
For Rick Building—For the man who shall Build his Master's Ricks for men over 25. 1st Prize £1, 2nd Prize 10s, 3rd Prize 5s. Four entries or 3rd Prize will be withheld.

CLASS 12.
For Thatching a rick of Corn or Hay not less than 10 tons. 1st Prize £1, 2nd Prize 10s, 3rd Prize 5s

All Entries for Classes 11 and 12 to be received by Monday, October 1st.

A Subscriber of 10s and upwards is entitled to compete for the prizes in Classes 4, 5 and 6. All teams to be entered on or before FRIDAY, OCTOBER 19th, 1928, and to be sent in by post to the Secretary. Teams to be in the Field at Half-past Eight o'clock, at which hour Tickets will be drawn. No Driver will be allowed to drive in any of the above Classes if having won a Prize. No assistance from Driver, this Rule will be strictly enforced. The Committee reserve to themselves the right to make any alterations that they may think fit.

Luncheon will be provided for the Committee and Subscribers only.

Dinner will be Provided at the Village Hall, High Ham

The President will take the Chair at 6.30 o'clock.   Tickets 4/- each.
E. KEEVIL, T. A. SHERRIN, Hon. Treasurers.   A. J. CULLEN, Hon. Sec.

The Herald Press, Langport.

Farming

The Ploughing Matches

"The Ploughing Matches were inland, on the higher ground, not on the moor. The soil on the moor is peat - black soil, very light - you never grew corn on it, mainly roots or kale. On the higher ground they grew corn. The ploughing matches were on Cook's land, or Keevil's, Maurice Vigar's, or at Wearne, Bowdens or at Farmer Jeans in Aller. Different people went, the doctor from Langport, Dr. Hesford, he went. People from all over, the ploughmen, their bosses, all the big people went, even if it was raining. There were no wellingtons in those days. There were boots and leggings."
Ron Tapscott

High Ham Ploughing Match, Carters' Class, 24 October 1913

"I went to watch the ploughing matches in the 1920s and 30s. There wasn't a very big crowd, mostly local people from Pitney, Aller and Wearne. All the horses were trimmed up with ribbons in their tails. There were several classes, the farmers' class, the farmers' sons, carters, and an open class for anyone from other districts. They were mostly at the end of October, beginning of November. People looked forward to it. Some women went too. They knew what was good ploughing!" Ron Tapscott

A ploughing competition with Joe Small (front) and Ted Gould (behind)

"There's the man who is the ploughman and then three horses and a driver. The driver led the back horse and had the reins for the front one. Once they got going, the horses would know exactly what to do. Our horse, Rock, went in the farmers' sons' or the farmers' class. The furrows had to be all even, they had to start in the middle, you had to be very accurate." Ron Tapscott

"Will Sherrin ploughed as a farmer's son, in about 1925. He won the silver watch - you couldn't win it twice. For many years Colonel Doddington put up the money for the prize, five guineas, for the watch. Dad's brother won the watch one year, 1906 or 1908. He won the watch, married Rose and then left for Canada. I've got it now. My Aunt Rose sent it to me after my uncle died." Ron Tapscott

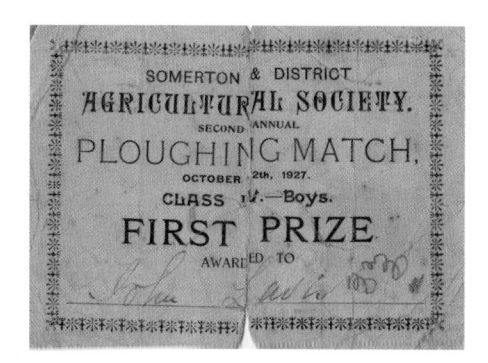

Somerton and District Agricultural Society Second Annual Ploughing Match, 12 October 1927. John 'Jack' Lavis won First Prize.

Henry Vigar, aged 14, competing in a ploughing match, 1937

"I could tell you about the ploughing competitions, we used to hold them at our farm. Then there were the ploughing meals. First the judges would have theirs, then the other men would have theirs." Joy Vigar (née Sherrin)

Horses

"It was quite an occasion when the stallion came in the spring. The man who had him was a small man. He would walk leading his stallion from Ilchester. Oh, I remember the stallion, he was so smart. He pranced, danced, it was like ballet. He had bells, his mane was tied with ribbons plaited into it. His tail was plaited with ribbons and the little man who brought him was so proud. He wouldn't be long at the farm. The mares might be interested, but they might not. If they weren't, then he'd go on somewhere else. But I always had to go into the house, I wasn't allowed to watch, but, of course, I used to peep out of the window! Not many people had mares they wanted served, but my Dad always did. At that time, in the 1930s a broken colt was making more than a cow. A cow would be about £20, a broken-in colt a lot more." [1] Peggy Coombes (née Vigar)

"My father bred horses and he broke them. They were Shire horses used for ploughing. My mother took care of the milking, my father made money from horses. They'd send for Dad to vet horses, if there was something wrong. Every year my father would sell three or four colts. People would come and buy them from him. It was word of mouth."
Peggy Coombes (née Vigar)

Jack Lavis' father, Charlie Lavis, with Plough Boy, which sold for £60 in 1918. Charlie Lavis lived at Rose Cottage, Bramwells and was a carter.

Les, Barbara and Fred Ford, Low Ham with Keevils' Bonnie, 1954

Ted Gould who worked for Mrs Carne-Hill, 1940s

"My father never had a tractor all his time. He had three teams and each team had three horses. He had a pony with a trap. He also had a cob, that was a bit heavier, that would go to milking. The milking was done by hand down on the moor. They used to drive to the cows with a bucket and a milk churn. That cob also used to do the horse mowing. At haymaking time, you had two horses that would mow the grass with a horse-drawn mower."
Joy Vigar (née Sherrin)

Tractors

"We didn't have a tractor till well after the war. It was a blue Standard Fordson. I can still remember the registration – GYA 460."
Rene Winter (née Webb)

Arthur Scriven, Low Ham, on Fordson Major tractor.[2]

Fred Ford and Standard Fordson tractor stuck in the snow, 30 December 1962

Andy Ford ploughing with Fordson Major tractor E27N, 1950s

Left to right: Andy and Fred Ford with Fordson Major tractor

"Barebones was the name of a field in Low Ham full of small stones, which made working it and growing anything difficult. My father put me at the age of about four on to a large flat-bed trailer behind the tractor, while he was doing some job in 'Barebones'. I rolled off the trailer while it was going along. I don't think it did me any harm thankfully, though it gave my father a shock to look round and see I had disappeared! There were real dangers on a farm as the tractor had no cab or roll-bars in those days. So my father was always at risk of a roll-over, which has killed a number of farm workers over the years." Stephen Julian Wheadon

Market Day

"Dad would go to Langport Market in his pony and trap. It was held every other Tuesday. Besides the auctioneers, there was the vet, seed reps, feed reps, and Bradfords was down by the station. Hill Seeds was at Bow House, Bow St, where Peppard's the funeral directors is now. The market sold calves and cows, some sheep, pigs and cattle. They used to hunt the cattle down to the bottom station to be transported to Yeovil, Taunton and elsewhere. Rolf Widdacombe, brother of Mrs Spearing, was one of the butchers who bought animals there. He was a butcher in Somerton. He would buy enough animals to butcher for a fortnight. Henry would bring the other animals not due for slaughter back here and keep them for a week. After Langport closed, Henry went to Highbridge with the cattle and sheep. The market was every Monday. There was also Yeovil on Mondays and Glastonbury on Tuesdays. Taunton had three market days, Tueday for fatstock, Thursday for special breeds, and Saturday was a general market with stallholders, plants, butter and cream, cakes and dressed poultry, and lots more." Joy Vigar (nee Sherrin)

"Father used to put on a collar and tie to go to Highbridge Market. He would spend most of the day there. It was like his day off." John Vigar

"Dad won the cup at the last Langport Fatstock Show Christmas c1961. He also came first that year at Highbridge with this Aberdeen Angus heifer. Dad showed at Highbridge, Yeovil, Bridgwater and Langport. He went on to show at Smithfield as well."
Les Inder

"Dad had milking cows, but his pride and joy was showing cattle. He won several cups. He also did market gardening, taking veg to Bristol, and he had a local fruit and veg round in the villages from the back of a pick-up. He was known for his cider which was made on the farm and people came from all over to drink Harry Inder's cider in 'The Cellar' at Gawlers Farm." Sheila Jewell (née Inder)

Langport Market Fatstock Show, 1961. Picture includes Les Inder, Toby Cobden, John Hill, Mr Hunt (Greenslade Taylor and Hunt) and Harry Inder holding cup with Mr Bond (Bond's Seeds, Somerton)

"I remember taking calves to Langport market, I took them in a pony and trap, two or three calves, you'd tie them to the front. Oh, they used to spruce themselves up to go to market, you'd never go in your working clothes, you'd be dressed up with a hat. I remember Father going to Yeovil market once and he saw a beautiful blue cow and he came home with it and said, 'What do you think of her? £100 she was'." Len Cox

"Bakers of Compton House were a transport firm in the 1950s and 60s. They used to take our calves to Taunton Market. They charged 5/- (25p) for each calf. They also sold petrol. The receipt we have for three months in 1963 was for 104 gallons. We paid £24 18s 4d. (approx £24.85)."
Ken and Jean Edmunds

"Before mains water was installed in Henley, how did the cows drink? Several local farmers took them down to the river near Bridge Farm where there was a drinking place. Twice a day you took them down to drink. We all had a set time otherwise the cows would have got mixed up!"
Len Cox

Sheep

Charles Hill, Dennis Davis' grandfather, shepherd at Hall Farm, High Ham.

"My grandfather used to send his dog home when it was dinnertime. Grandma used to make up his sandwiches, tie them round the dog's neck and then send him back to Grandad." Dennis Davis

The Church in the Field, Low Ham with Cooks' sheep grazing

"We had Dorset Horns and Hampshire Downs. We had between three and four hundred, which was a lot of sheep in those days, the 1940s and 50s. Some went to Bridgwater Fair, others to Taunton Market or occasionally Langport or Ilminster. They grazed the grass around the church in Low Ham. Dad wouldn't keep cows for this purpose round the church for obvious reasons. We'd lamb the end of December into January so they would be ready for the Easter market. Before shearing, they were taken to Pitney Harbour[3] to be washed ready for shearing. They were dipped in Low Ham. I used to rear the orphan lambs."
Molly Cullen (née Cook)

Peggy feeding a suck lamb, 1941

"Not very many people kept sheep around this area. My father was one of the few that did, that was at Roman Farm in Park. He had about 20 to 30 cows in the 1940s and about 50 sheep, but not many of the farms had sheep and it wasn't the intensive farming that there is today. I remember when I was a child I enjoyed feeding the suck lambs, the orphan lambs. We just used an ordinary bottle and a goose quill about three inches long. We bandaged the quill to the top of the bottle and made a sort of teat with a rag. It worked fine. We would wash it all out and it lasted the life of a lamb. I remember the Sherrin brothers in Henley had a mobile shearing machine. I used to turn the handle. It had a big wheel and the cogs drove the clippers. The wool was quite valuable then." Peggy Coombes (née Vigar)

Harold Vigar sheep shearing with his children, Henry and Peggy, 1946

Milking

Harry Inder milking, 1930s

"My mother did the milking. When the milk prices dropped in the 1930s, there was a revolt. Many farmers threw their milk away in disgust, they wouldn't sell it at such low prices. Then the Milk Marketing Board was formed and everyone got the same price, a reasonable price."
Peggy Coombes (née Vigar)

"We used to milk about seven to ten cows, depending if they were dry or in calf. Everyone was milking three or four or more. The milk lorry used to stop at every farm and pick up two or more milk churns. There were up to 30 small farms in Henley alone." Rene Winter (née Webb)

"I can remember going down on the moor with my milking stool in all winds and weathers. They used to come round and collect the milk every day. We used to put out two milk churns for them at the bottom of the drove. After the evening milking we used to stand the churns in the rhyne to keep them cool." Edna Webb (née Sherrin)

Molly Cullen milking Spider, 1950

"In the summer we'd take the three-legged stools. I remember coming home from school and Dad was milking and I'd change my clothes and go and milk a few cows. Nearly everyone milked."
Rene Winter (née Webb)

Linda Lavis coming back from milking with her father, 1920s

From left: Den Scriven, Joe Groves, Des Groves and Vera Scriven at Park Farm Dairy

"In the 1950s milking was still largely done by hand, but it may have been an automated milking system was put in as time went by. The milk was taken across from the milking shed to the dairy, where it was poured into large metal churns. These metal churns were then hauled up on to a platform outside the dairy and adjacent to the road, where the milk lorry would come to collect them. A portion of the milk would have been taken for our household use, so we always had fresh milk. I enjoyed rounding up the cows for milking. They were used to the daily routine of trotting from the field to the farm and into the cowstalls. I would help muck out after milking, scraping up the dung and putting it on the heap (to be used later in the dung-spreader on the fields), hosing down the stalls, putting fresh hay for fodder etc. The cows were like family."
Stephen Julian Wheadon

Butter and Cheese Making

Metal double cheese press with moulds for both Caerphilly and Cheddar, at Charity Farm [4]

Old wooden cheese press from Decoy Farm

"We made Caerphilly in the winter. It only took three hours to ripen and was mature in two to three months. Cheddar we made in spring and summer with that flush of milk. It took five to six hours till ripe and six to twelve months before mature." Ethel Webb

"Mother took the butter on the back of a bicycle. She went to Long Sutton and Langport. She went straight to the shopkeeper. It was a type of butter they couldn't get and people fancied it. We didn't have Friesian cows, we had Shorthorns, better milk. The butter in the 1930s came from New Zealand. It came in big blocks to the shopkeeper and he cut it and potted it up. People, when they tasted Mother's butter, rather liked it. New Zealand butter had to have some preservatives in it, local butter didn't." Ron Tapscott

"There was a little cubby hole in the dairy at Henley Farm. You opened it up and there was a board with a rope through it and that went upstairs. You put your cheese on it, wound the handle and it went up, where there was someone to pull it in, then put the cheese in the storeroom. I had to turn them every other day. During the war the Ministry of Food would come and grade them and take them away. Before the war they were taken to Highbridge Market by horse and cart." [5]
Ethel Webb

"When milk prices dropped in the thirties, we didn't throw away our milk, my mother made cheese then. She had been a cheese maker before she was married. She made it for us and sold a bit. That was the only time we made cheese."
Peggy Coombes (née Vigar)

Pigs and Poultry

"When the boar came to serve the sow my grandfather would say, 'You maidens, go inside.' We weren't allowed to watch. I expect we were all peeping." Margaret Porter (née Webb)

"Everyone had a pig, which ate all the food waste. My parents kept several pigs and I remember Mother cooking vegetable peelings and mixing it with cereal and giving it to the pigs. When a litter was born, they would sell them on, keeping just one or two for ourselves." Brian Hill

Anna McCallion with the pig in the orchard at Hillborne House, early 1960s

"Mr. Bartlett was the pig killer. He had one of those girt pig horses. It's like a big wooden slab, like a table with arms at each end. He would come and do the business, kill it and take out all the innards and then hang it. Then he would come back a couple of days later and dress it."
Margaret Porter and Ethel Webb

"We always kept a pig, killed it, salted it, we kept it by salting it. The killing wasn't anything particular, just something that happened."
Ron Tapscott

"Pigs were killed at home by Charlie Bartlett who worked for Willie Calder, a Langport butcher. It was a great help having a pig during the war, but it wasn't always easy to get enough ration food for the pig. When your pig was killed your meat ration was cancelled by the Food Office for a number of weeks according to the number of people in the household." Guy Tapscott

"I liked the pigs, better than a horse or a cow. I hated the killing. I don't eat much meat. We used to go and feed the little pigs. We used to love that." Linda Lavis (née Gould)

"Poultry was quite useful. Mother sold poultry. Eggs were mainly for ourselves. We didn't sell many eggs." Ron Tapscott

"In the forties when I was about 15, I did nothing for weeks except pick blackberries. It was the school holidays. I would get up early in the morning, it was lovely weather. There was a big demand for blackberries. They were using them for dye, so it didn't matter what state they were in. A chap came with a big cider butt and I'd fill it with blackberries. I earned enough money that summer to buy my own fowl house. It was on wheels. I wanted to keep poultry myself. I could also buy my own chicks, and I did, 50 at a time."
Peggy Coombes (née Vigar)

Elizabeth Ann Inder in the orchard opposite the Memorial Hall. Houses were built there in the 1960s.

Everyday Farm Work

February 1931. Page from work diary of Will Sherrin [6]

"The most was about seven cows, nobody had more than eight. There were always a couple of dry cows, a couple calving, and you had pigs. During the war we only had two pigs, that was all you were allowed to kill then. We'd have a few sheep, chickens and ducks. We had two or three heavy horses for farm work and a lighter horse for the cart. People always helped each other out, especially like haymaking time. Our father used to do drilling for others as well as his own farm work. The lambs and calves were taken to Langport Market. They used to bring cattle in by train in those cattle trucks. That was at the bottom station. Father got a new hay elevator and it was delivered by train. He picked it up and drove it up through Langport and then on home. He used his horses then as he didn't have a tractor." Ethel Webb and Rene Winter (née Webb)

Fred and Frank Keevil, Old Manor Farm, Low Ham, 1920s

Henry Tapscott, with Rock, c1950
"Rock was about my age, he was a colt when I was young."
Ron Tapscott

"In the 1920s there was a smith at Low Ham, Charlie Keevil, but most went to Lucas, out Pitney."
Recounted at gathering of family and friends at Margaret Porter's house.

"Henry and his father probably went to Somerton to shoe horses, because they took their milk there every day to the milk factory. I think it was Mr George Nutt who was the smith there. Later, after the war they went to Pitney to Kurt Neumann (Newman). There was also a blacksmith next to the chapel in Langport. Mr Trout was the smith."
Joy Vigar (née Sherrin)

Sheila Jewell, brother Leslie and their mother in their cart. The horse was named Jubilee since it was born in Jubilee Year 1937.

Charlie Webb and Des Groves fodder beet harvesting with the dogs, Fido and Towser

"We had all sorts of things. It was an ordinary smallholding in the twenties. We used to sell things to anybody who needs it."
Linda Lavis (née Gould)

"My father had a drill for mangolds and he would go drilling for other people. We'd go to the market at Langport and Highbridge."
Rene Winter (née Webb)

"In the 1950s I used to pull the mangolds, lay them in rows after tea of an evening. The next day they would come and chop off the greens, then they would be picked up and put in the putt, tipped in a heap, then covered in hay and kept for winter feed. The tops were picked up and then fed to the cows. Nothing was wasted."
Edna Webb (née Sherrin)

"It was good to have land out on the moor because, after a dry summer, the high ground was very dry and not very useful, but it was green out here on the low moor land."
Guy Tapscott

Beans, Peas and Potatoes

"We always grew some potatoes, some for ourselves and some to sell." Ron Tapscott

"We used to grow about an acre and a half of potatoes. Some were for ourselves, but the bulk were sold locally. We used to take a lot to the bra factory in Somerton for their canteen. I used to have to sort and grade them before they were bagged." Val Scriven (née Webb)

Arthur and Andrew Scriven and Ken Mitchell planting potatoes in the 1960s

Collecting potatoes at Stembridge, Jack Cullen on right

Pea picking in 1956/57. The gypsies camped at Gawlers Farm, Long Street and were employed by Harry Inder for seasonal work.

"They used to come up over the hill with their wagons. They used to double up sometimes and put an extra horse in front to help get over the last bit. In the road one of the horses slipped down and, before you could stop it, the wagon was pulling the horse backwards and got badly dragged up on the tarmac. My mum ran out to the gypsy bloke and she gave him vinegar and brown paper. He washed it all out with vinegar and bandaged the horse's legs up with the paper. They came to pick beans, peas, potatoes and then apples for cider. They'd all come and then they'd all go every year."
Brian Hill

"The bit of road with the wide verge between Wood Farm and the bungalow at the junction to Pitney and Park was always used by the gypsies every year. They would pull up their wagons and horses there by the side of the road. They would be going pea or potato picking at the farms around."
Val Scriven (née Webb)

Haymaking

Will Loader mowing grass for hay, 1930s

"This was Will Loader mowing grass for hay. The Loaders used to do mowing for other people. We all had horses. I used to mow like that, with two horses. You can see the tool box in the back, for the wrenches and fitments. We all had small farms, some people didn't have the machine or the horses. There wasn't any need to go to the expense of getting a mowing machine if you only had five or ten acres. Dad used to go round mowing in his younger day." Ron Tapscott

Lunchtime in the fields, 1920s

"There was the time when it was haymaking. It seemed as if everyone was out with a pitchfork turning hay. We were evacuated here and even my mother, a Londoner, was expected to turn out."
Irene Stimpson (née Figg)

"Oh, in the summer we would all do the milking when they were haymaking. We used to take them whole dinners - potatoes, gravy, carry it all out to them. Woe betide you if you forgot the gravy!"
Ethel Webb and Rene Winter (née Webb)

Hayman Scriven at Old Manor Farm, Low Ham about to go out with the hay rake, 1930s

William 'Buffer' Ford's last haymaking, July 1942 [7]

"Farm work was hard and poorly paid in the fifties. There was one Fordson Major tractor, a trailer, harrows, a roller and a dung spreader. I think the hay-baler may have been hired in at the required times. There was no elevator to raise the bales of hay. My father pitched bales with a long-handled fork, no mean feat from the ground to the top of the trailer. When I was old enough, I went on the trailer to do the stacking of the bales. I enjoyed haymaking time, working with the men and feeling quite grown up and useful." Stephen Julian Wheadon

Harvesting

The Keevil brothers harvesting wheat, New Manor Farm, Low Ham, 1920s/30s

"We used to grow our own corn. We took it to Somerton to the millers to be ground into flour. Mother then weighed it up and gave it to the baker. He used to come round in his pony and trap with a hood. He was in the village, Mr Lockyer was his name. He cooked your bread with your own flour. That was in the 1920s and the 30s." Linda Lavis (née Gould)

"We had to grow some wheat and we had it ground. We sold most of it as corn and kept some for our own use. It was usually ground at Somerton, sometimes at Othery. We took down a whole sack and had it ground. That was up to the 1940s." Ron Tapscott

Binding at Cook's Farm, Low Ham, 1953

First combine harvester in the parish at Old Manor Farm with John Cook driving and Charlie Scriven bagging, c1956. [8]

Thrashing[9]

John Cooksley's threshing machine. *"You always needed a half a ton of steam coal per day for a good thrashing. We used to go and watch them threshing at dinnertime from school."* Ron Tapscott

"Bert Bown looked after the new threshing machine. It was Cook's who got it during the war or just after. It was pulled by a tractor, which ran off petrol /TVO. The threshing machine ran off a belt from the tractor. It was an American Case tractor, it was supplied by America under the War Lease or Lend Scheme. They'd put in the corn and it would separate the corn from the straw. As a kid I used to follow it around. It was good fun because towards the end, there were plenty of rats and the dogs would chase them." Dennis Davis

"When the old man went to start the tractor one day the handle came out, you started them with a handle then. That day he wasn't quick enough and it flew out and hit him in the face and broke his jaw." Doug Bown

"There was a thatcher called Fisher. He lived next to where the Agricentre is now. He thatched the hayricks and the corn mows. He went gadding as well, which is pollarding the willow trees." Joy Vigar (née Sherrin)

Harvesting at Old Manor Farm, 1923

Cider Making

"In the 1910s and later my father had three orchards and some beautiful apples - Pearmains, Scarlet Seedling, Tom Putt, Quentino, Blenheim Orange and many more kinds. He used to pay an old lady we called Smacker threepence a bag to pick up the cider apples to grind into cider. I used to like to go out where the cider was made and have a glass of cider and a wheat straw to draw it through and drink it like that. The men used to come in and have bread and cheese and raw onions with salt and eat it with their pocket knives." Lena Kingston (née Hoare)[10]

"People with the best cider had the best labourers for haymaking. Workers knew who made the best cider." Guy Tapscott

Top left: Bill Dean holding a cider jug, c1960; Top right: Cider making at Nenmead Farm, High Ham. Picture includes Cliff Crossman, 'Hacky' Crossman, Bert Wheadon, Jack Lavis

Bottom left to right: the cider cheese ready to press - Jack Cox and son Len, 1963; Margaret Cox shovelling the apples into the mill for the cider, 1963 at Tutnell, Henley; in the cider barn at Nenmead Farm: Brian Chubb, Bill Buckland, Joan Buckland, Peggy Lawrence, Gwen Chubb, 'Hacky' Crossman, Bert Wheadon, Jimmy Upham

Hunting...

"It was the Seavington Hunt around here in the 1950s and 60s, they met in High Ham up at Vigar's and in Low Ham, a few times a year. Lady Berkeley had hounds at Field House, where the Madgwicks live now. She had 14 couples. Archie Peppard had six couples. We would go out on a Saturday, on horseback. It was rough and ready up to Turn Hill and out on the moors and to Aller. It was fun. It was part and parcel of farming life." [11]
Molly Cullen (née Cook)

Meet of the Seavington Hunt at Netherham Farm, Low Ham, 1950s

"I hunted with the Seavington Hunt. You could get about three days hunting a fortnight, if you didn't mind doing the distance. The Seavington Hunt went as far as the edge of the Poldens. You had to hack to the meets, sometimes it could be ten miles. Before I had a trailer, the furthest I went hacking was One Elm, that's beyond Martock. You didn't think anything of it, and you used to ride back when it was getting dark. I'd be wearing a black coat and be on a black horse, no lights and nearly dark, but there was hardly any traffic. Life was quite different then."
Rosemary Oram (née Wylie)

"I used to go out hunting with Archie Peppard. There were a few of us. I used to ride a pony Archie had bought at Bridgwater Fair for five pounds as the horse only had one eye. Archie had the horn and wore the red coat. He was a proper huntsman, he loved it. He had quite a few hounds, the old ones from Seavington Hunt. We'd go off through Aller Woods and the hounds would drive the fox towards the guns, which were round the den and then they would shoot it."
Les Inder

From left to right: Brian Hill, Mervyn Cook and Michael Bown holding up a fox

Digging out a fox in either Garston or Ashwell field just beyond Low Ham Church

... Shooting and Fishing

"Because there was a shortage of fresh eggs and things after the war, the boys would go climbing trees in the spring. I can recall going down to Fir Tree Farm and the boys climbed up and got the eggs from the crows and rooks. They were for eating. I never ate them."
Molly Cullen (née Cook)

"My favourite was baked starlings, but they took a long time to prepare. We had to pick all the feathers off and Mother had to draw the insides and stuff and roast them. Another time, when it had been raining, my father would go down to the river and catch eels. Then we had to skin them, and what a slimy job that was. I had to have a bucket of wood ash and put the eels in to skin them. That was another delicious meal when Mum used to fry them. That was in the 1920s."
Lena Kingston (née Hoare)[10]

"We caught eels when it was thundery weather. The river would be quite high. We went down with the tin bath and a pole through the two handles. We put that in the river. We'd have this rayball, a ball of worms on the end of a long stick which you use as a fishing rod. When you could feel the eel biting, you pulled, not too quickly, and heaved it over the bath, gave it a bit of a shake and the eel would drop off into the bath." Ron Tapscott

Austin Webb outside Wood Farm, Park, having just shot a fox that had been raiding the chicken run, 1930s.

"Rabbits was one of the staple foods. Dad used to go shooting rabbits and pheasants. He kept lurcher dogs and used to go hare coarsing. He shot foxes, he kept a lot of chickens, so shot foxes when they got in his chicken house." Dennis Davis

"We went up Bowdens by Crossman's (Nenmead Farm). There were hundreds and hundreds of pigeons up there and we'd go shooting up there. That's what we had to live on in those days, the forties and fifties, pigeons and rabbits." Charlie Webb

Amy Ford holding a locally caught eel, 1960s

Water and Electricity

"We all had wells and some had pumps before the water was piped in.[1] People would never build a house until the diviner had been and found a well they could draw from." Guy Tapscott

Carrying water from the well with yoke and pails, c1920

"We used to have six people coming in here to Henley Corner House for water. I remember Uncle Sid Vigar used to come up every night with a yoke and two buckets on chains until the mid-1930s. They got water for drinking tea and that. For washing they took it off the roof or out of the river. You couldn't use well-water for washing, only rain water. It was too hard, you couldn't get the soap to work with it. We had the bath in front of the fire. When I was haymaking I got very black. I'd wash twice, then the water would go for the garden. In the summer I'd put buckets of water outside with glass on top and the sun heated it up." Ron Tapscott

"My sister and I visited the Rectory quite often before the war, and were evacuated there for the first eight or nine months of the war. I think water was pumped into the Rectory kitchen by a hand pump, but I don't know what other water was in the house. Lighting was by paraffin lamps downstairs, probably candles upstairs, with small 'Aladdin' night light paraffin lamps down a long corridor to the back bedrooms where my sister and I were." [2] Arthur Robinson

"When I was evacuated the primitive conditions were a very big shock to me. The toilet was a shed half-way down a long garden and the waste went into a pit below. Water was drawn from a pump on the opposite side of the road. A primus stove was used to cook on and an oven was part of the coal fire for cooking cakes and roasting. An oil lamp was used to light the main room in the evening, and a candle to go upstairs and get into bed. One incident I recall is that of going outside to the pump to draw some water. No one told me that in order for water to come up one had to pour a little water down. I must have got fed up pumping away and no water coming up. I swore at it!" Alma Vinter (née Willoughby)

"Well-head in the garden of Walnut Cottage, High Ham. Similar ones also at Cottage on The Green and Hall Farm, High Ham, and Southways, Low Ham." [3] Mrs Williams

Water pump, Henley Farm [3]

Gares Cottage, Low Ham, 5 July 1952. Fetching water from the well.
Left to right: Maureen and Sheila Scriven, Vera, Alma and Amy Ford

"When we lived down Henley, we got water out of a dipping – there was no well. Charlie put two rings round so the animals didn't get in there. The people in Stout got theirs from it too."
Frances Webb (née Weech)

Digging a well at Stembridge Lea, October 1962

"When I came home from school my first job was to get two buckets from the well, which was at the other end of the garden, and bring them down and put them in the kitchen for my mother because she didn't have running water. She had a copper for washing with one of those old slipper baths in the wash house because a lot of people had wash houses in those days. Hillcrest was the first place in the village to have running water and a flush toilet." Dennis Davis

Two-seater privy ('bucket and chuck it'), Mill Cottage, Stembridge Mill [4]

"We had a bucket toilet up the top of the garden. Dad had this big crater where he used to empty the bucket toilet and put some dirt over it. I suppose that's where the rhubarb was going eventually, because everyone said they used to put custard on theirs, but we didn't."
Brian Hill

"At Jubilee Cottage our toilet was up the end of the garden path. One of us girls would have to stand at the back door and shine the torch up to show the way. At night or a wet day we would sit and cut up newspapers, put a little hole through and then string them up and put them on the back of the lavy door. When they cleaned it out, Mum or Dad used to have to dig a hole in the garden and bury it."
Gwen Chubb (née Bown)

Two-holer at Furlong House Farm, demolished in the 1980s

Chairman of High Ham Parish Council, Mr Lionel Cook, switching on the electricity, Low Ham, 1952

"Henry's mother and father down at Park, they had their own generator. When Henry and I got married we lived in the red house in Parksy. In the farmhouse they had a storage of 50 watts and that was done with four 12-volt batteries. Henry's father had the electric put into Parksy. There was two 25-volt batteries. The generator was used for milking. I could only use an iron when the engine was running."
Joy Vigar (née Sherrin)

"We used to go upstairs with a candle. That was the only light we had, we had oil lamps, but they were more dangerous. We had candles. Violet used to have one right by her bed and how she never ever caught fire I'll never know because she used to have clothes all around her. She had a candle till she were quite old." Linda Lavis (née Gould)

"We had oil lamps which used to always smell. You could open the door and it was like when people had gas, you'd walk in the house and know instantly that people had paraffin lamps or candles or whatever."
Brian Hill

"We moved to Hillcrest after the war. We had pressure lamps and an oil stove to cook chips on and one of the best Christmas cakes I ever made. My husband Vic bought a two-burner stove with an oven on the top. You could turn the oil down low for hours to cook the cake. I can remember it now, it was a lovely cake." Una Dyer

"It changed our lives having the electricity and water, although a lot of the cottages down through here still use the water from the Roman villa – the spring there. That water was used for the baths. We call it Cook's Water. The pressure wasn't enough for us to have a bathroom, but we had piped Cook's Water in the kitchen. The local council, the County Councillor Mr Burcham, the Electricity Board man and all the village gathered round. It was dark so we could switch the lights on at the electricity pole outside Dairy House Farm. Mr Clark and Mr Cook switched it on, being the two local farmers down Low Ham. The electricity was switched on, but it was a long time before we had it in the house." Gwen Chubb (née Bown)

First electric pole in Low Ham, 17 May 1951. Fred Ford with Keevil's dog

Trades and Other Work

Robert Charles Davis at Ham Court. He started as a groom in 1912 and worked his way up to be Mrs Carne-Hill's 'right-hand man'.

Robert Charles Davis with Ham Court cook/housekeeper, Mrs Knowles (far right)

Postcard written by Frances Biggs who worked as a domestic servant at Ham Court. Transcript below:

"are quite well so now dear Lily I must say I am a lot better at present but Mrs (Carne Hill of Ham Court) will not let me do much work yet she has the nurse in every other day to look at it but I am sorry to say I have got some on my right leg the nurse told me I don't know what to do so I think I must bring this to an end with my best love to all from your truly Frances Biggs."

Frances married Hayman Scriven in 1911.

"The young Joe Small was a 'strapper' [1] - someone who went 'strapping', self-employed, doing all sorts of things, like thrashing, haymaking, hoeing and ditch-clearing. There were probably a dozen 'strappers' in the parish in the 1920s. I used to work ditching and rhyning in the 1960s. Farming was becoming more intensive and we had a field here and a field there, and it was less viable, so I went ditching and thrashing for other people. Well, if anyone wanted help you were the first one they asked. With ditching, or 'rhyning', they used to ask you to tender for the job. It depended on the rhyne, if it was a bad one you charged more. You put in a price per 'rope'. A 'rope' [2] was 20 feet. That was a measurement used for clearing ditches, rhynes and rivers and it was certainly used up to the 1980s. There was always plenty of paid work clearing ditches, rhynes and rivers in the winter." Ron Tapscott

"There were two shoemakers in Ham. Adolphus Gooding lived near the pub - the cottages aren't there any more. He went on till about 1920. Walter Priddle made shoes and boots in my time, until the 1930s - good waterproof hand-sewn leather boots. Even when wellingtons came we didn't get them for a long time. I remember my first pair, I paid 30 shillings, a whole week's wages for a farmworker, in the mid-1930s." Ron Tapscott

"Ted Priddle's father was the cobbler, he mended shoes, made and repaired harnesses and saddles, he was a saddleman. He also maintained the village pump. He could do anything. He was a maintenance man of sorts.
Mr Lavis was the wheelright, he lived and worked in Bonds Farm, (now Windsor Grove Farm). He made wagons, he repaired them and he also bonded the wheels - they were bonded to the metal band on the wheel, put on the forge and the metal beaten to the wheel. Mr Lavis was also an undertaker and made coffins."
Peggy Coombes (née Vigar)

Mr Frank Lavis with his two apprentices at Bonds Farm, Long Street, 1912. He was the last wheelwright and smith in the parish and carried on his business till 1940. The wagon was one of two made for Mr W J Cullen for export to New Zealand where he had emigrated from Coombe.[3]

Left: Luther Andrew George Crossman, stonemason. Taken on Albert Crossman's wedding day in 1920. Right: Frank Loader, carpenter and son William, tree feller

"I used to cut a lot of stone and in the last few years a lot of big paving stones. That's all there was around here long ago, a lot of quarries and a lot of stone crackers around here.[4] They used to sit by the side of the road and they'd bring along a load of stone and they would crack them into pieces. I was an apprentice to a stone cutter and worked up Bancombe Road, went on my bicycle. Used to dress all the tools – come Friday night I used to ride to Sutton to the blacksmith, leave the tools, then the next week go up with another lot, leave them and bring the others back all ready, sharp for the next week. I cut all the stone for Henry Vigar's wall." Charlie Webb

"Hacky Crossman dug graves and emptied privies on Saturday mornings. He used to put the contents of ours under Granny's cabbages next door, at Hillborne. He wouldn't empty one chap's privy, because he still called himself Colonel although he wasn't in the army any more, and Hacky Crossman disapproved of that." Anna McCallion

Jimmy Allen dealt in poultry and calves, and anything else he could buy and sell, 1920s

"I went to work in the shop after I left school, then my auntie came down and said I had to have a proper job. I didn't work all day there. She said, 'I know a job for you, you can come up to London'. Well of course I jumped for it, didn't I. My mother didn't really want me to go, but I said I was going anyway. So I went up to London and she said, 'You've got to say you're 19 mind'. I were only 17." Linda Lavis (née Gould)

"My mother sewed, she learnt dressmaking, she was an apprentice with Joy Vigar's mother in Mrs Spearing's house." Dennis Davis

"The cottages near the pub, which are gone now, used to be lived in by glovers [5] - the women would sit in their doorways or in their windows stitching gloves which were collected and paid for weekly." Bill Westcott

"Mum (Grace Inder) learnt gloving at the Langport glove factory which was in Bow Street.[5] She made gloves at home. My grandfather bought her a gloving machine as a wedding present so she could earn money. She made gloves up to the time she was 80. They were given the leather cut out and ready to sew. She made a pair of gloves for the Queen. I can't remember the year - she didn't make a big thing about it. I learnt glove making from my mother when I was about 15. I worked as an outworker for firms in Street, Westbury and Burfields of Martock." Sheila Jewell (née Inder)

"I used to work for my grandmother at Huish Episcopi Friday nights and help grandfather Saturday mornings with vegetables to take to Langport and help to sell them. Then I used to come back and have dinner midday and clean up Grandmother's house in the afternoon and walk home, which was about four miles. When I lost my husband I did everything I could possibly do - sewing, washing, pea-picking for farmers, potato-picking for farmers and everything where I could earn a shilling to get round. It didn't hurt me and I like outdoor work." Amy Ford [6]

"During the war I worked at Westlands. Mostly we got a ride in Mr. Hale's car, but they wanted us to work Saturdays and Sundays. He didn't work weekends, so we cycled to Yeovil, we started at seven in the morning and finished at six at night. It used to be an hour and a half to cycle. I had icicles in my hair in the winter, and on frosty mornings it was a job to keep on the bike as there were very icy roads. I passed out a few times because of the cold." Frances Webb (née Weech)

"When I left school, I started work in Clarks, Street. I went in the wages office 'cos I was good at maths. I was 15. I was too young to do a full week, so I used to go Wednesday afternoons and Friday mornings to Strode College. Clarks paid me £2 12s 6d a week. I worked at Clarks till 1959 when I got married. Then I went to work at Leffman's, the bra factory in Somerton. I worked on the machines, then I was a trainee manager. I trained all the young ones to use the machines. I was scared to death they were going to catch their fingers." Gwen Chubb (née Bown)

"After I finished school, I started work at Kelways.[7] Vera, Rita and Alma Ford were already working there. A bell would ring four times a day, early morning and lunch time and again at the end of the day, calling workers in and out. The bell was on the left of the entrance arch and was rung manually by the caretaker. I worked there for two years. I cycled there in the morning, back home for lunch, then back again for the afternoon." Shirley Badman (née Hill)

"Millfield took the Old Rectory over in the late 1950s, early 60s.[8] The house was very run down by then as the vicar had moved into the Rectory. Mr and Mrs Reed were houseparents. My granny, Frances Moore, worked as a cook there, and Mrs Fisher, Mrs Lavis, Mrs Atkins, Sheila Perry, Primrose Purchase. My mum was kitchen help and did little jobs around the place. She worked in the evenings. She would see large cars with chauffeurs coming up the drive dropping off the boys and their belongings. The boys were often tearful and homesick and she would take them into the kitchen and give them cups of tea and comfort them." Brian Hill

"1958 I left school at 15 on the Friday and started work on the Monday at John Snows in Glastonbury, working on the machines, cycling seven miles each way. I stayed 18 months. Then I went to Morlands, in the pram canopy section, in the engineering department. Flowery material was added at Morlands in Highbridge. These were for Prestige Prams." Mike Jenkins

Provisions, Pub, Policeman and Nurse

The first High Ham Post Office run by the Lavis family (outside Wheelwrights), c1900

"My aunt told me that about 1890 George Clapp used to walk from Langport with the post, delivering on the way, and when he'd finished he had a hut behind the church in High Ham and he used to stay there and sell stamps, he was there until three o'clock. People would bring him their post, he WAS the post box, he'd take the letters back to Langport, walk back. Then the Post Office got mechanised! - there were bicycles! The Lavis family started the Post Office probably between 1895 and 1900. This is a picture of it. They were a big family."
Ron Tapscott

"Around the time the Post Office was on The Green Miss Perrin ran a shop at Hillborne House and she married Orlando Lavis, that would have been in the early 1900s. When his wife died, Orlando Lavis had the shop and then he went to Highbridge and he let let the shop to Mrs Mears. The shop was run by Mrs Mears and her daughter and then they took over the Post Office as well. So then the Post Office went to Hillborne." Ron Tapscott

High Ham Post Office at Hillborne, early 1900s. Jo Lavis (2nd left), Mrs Mears, Ted Priddle (far right)

"About the time of the First World War Rector Crossman retired and no longer needed his coachman's house and Mrs Mears bought it and transferred the Post Office there (now Laburnum House). Then after this Mr Hunt came on the scene. He had left the army and had a job as a travelling salesman and went around the district selling groceries, anything that shops required, and that's how he met Miss Mears, and they got married and he took over the Post Office and shop. That's how the Post Office came to be on The Green." Ron Tapscott

"I was born in 1912 at Fountain. You never put any addresses on the envelopes, the postman knew everyone. He came on a bicycle when I was a child, he delivered the post at about eight o'clock in the morning and he came again at four o'clock to clear the letterbox and deliver any other post. He used to come into us, my mother would make him a cup of tea and he would sort through all the mail he had to deliver and he'd decide if he wanted to deliver it that afternoon or not, he could tell from the envelope if it was important I suppose, and if he didn't think it was he would say, 'That can wait till tomorrow'." Freda Hayes (née Cullen)

"The Post Office was run by an old lady, Mrs Mears, when I was a young child and when she got too old it was run by her daughter. She got married to Percival Hunt, a travelling salesman, and then they ran it and it became known as Hunt's. Mr Hunt revitalised it. Mrs Mears used to wear a long black skirt, all women over about 40 seemed to, I don't remember hearing anything about Mr Mears. Women in those days had no shape, their clothes just hung off them. I don't remember Mrs Mears ever appearing in public apart from being in the shop and going to church. Women in those days seemed to get married and never leave the house. I often think about that, it was quite amazing, but they didn't go out much. My grandmother, Jane Ford, she lived near us, and she had a black bonnet for church - in the summer she put artificial violets in it and in the winter a plume of black feathers."
Freda Hayes (née Cullen)

"The Hunts' shop was the Post Office as well, it was in the big house on the corner. You went in the front there by the post box. They sold everything, they had clothes and all sorts of things, food, everything. My mother sold them butter to sell in the shop. I used to clean up and bag up the sugar, they used to have it in these big sacks. I didn't serve in the shop, I wasn't good enough for that!"
Linda Lavis (née Gould)

Hunts shop and Post Office, The Green High Ham, 1965

"The Hunts sold absolutely everything, paraffin, cheese, butter, coal, shoes, boots. I used to always be fascinated during the war watching Mr Hunt when he was putting up the groceries, because butter, as you know, was strictly rationed, and cutting a piece off, he used to have about a quarter of a pound piece of butter, but I used to think how wonderful it was at how accurate he was at cutting it off. Absolutely precise." Dennis Davis

"We came down and bought Ham Court. I was about 22. I loved horses, horses were a bit out of fashion in the 1940s and 50s. I'd just learnt to drive so I did go into Langport to do shopping, but you didn't need to go shopping much, fish came in vans and the Hunts were very good, if they didn't have something you wanted, they would get it for you. The post arrived at seven in the morning, delivered to your door, there were two deliveries a day." Rosemary Oram (née Wylie)

Mr and Mrs Hunt, 1960s

"We loved Mr Hunt's window decorations - they were priceless! We were always curious and we used to make a detour to go and see them on our way to school. If it was raining there would just be a pair of wellington boots and an umbrella, and I remember once a cardboard box with the lid just slightly open with a pink lacy bit of underwear peeping out and a notice saying 'Enquire Within'! He had a good sense of humour and he used the window to sell his goods, what you could buy in the shop or what he could get for you. His displays varied from day to day sometimes, with the weather and the season. If it went suddenly cold there would be a pair of long-johns - men's combinations - or a hot water bottle. If there was a heatwave you'd find a picnic basket or parasol or a deckchair." Peggy Coombes (née Vigar)

"Oh, Mr Hunt's shop it was wonderful, you could get everything, I remember going in once to buy Dad a cap, he said 'Get me size 6 ⅞'. Well I brought home three hats, a size 6, a size 7 and a size 8! You could get long-john pants, socks, scarves, gloves, hats and obviously the grocery side, stamps and pensions, towels, sheets. Anything he didn't have and you'd asked for he would write down and I guarantee that next week he'd have it. He used to close the shop of a Wednesday and that was the time he went to the wholesalers. He had a little A40 car and he used to load that little car right up." Gwen Chubb (née Bown)

The Green, High Ham, showing Laburnum House before Hunts Post Office moved there. In the distance is the building (now demolished) at Hillborne where there was the shop run by Mr Lavis, then Mrs Mears and lastly, Mr & Mrs Spearing.

"Mr Spearing was a lovely man he could do any sort of job, and carpentry. Mrs Spearing ran the shop. It was always there when I were a girl. She used to sell lots of comics and different things, sweets, groceries, ham… He used to do carpentry and different things, that's why there is that big place at the back." Linda Lavis (née Gould)

"Mrs Spearing sold cigarettes and baccy, matches and some groceries, but the other side of the shop was the DIY store with paintbrushes, paint, glue, and also Mr Spearing had wallpaper books to choose your wallpaper. Hunts was more clothes – stockings, scarves, gloves. And I think Mrs Spearing used to buy the blackberries too."
Shirley Sparks (née Lavis)

"I remember the Spearings' shop, it was opposite the school. There were two shops, the Hunts ran the Post Office and Mr and Mrs Spearing ran the shop that sold sweets. I remember when I was young in the late 1950s, they had so many jars, we used to buy penny chews, black jacks, lollypops, gobstoppers, sherbert dips, aniseed balls, oh, and sweet cigarettes, do you remember those, in packets, and they had red tips."
Gary Mitchell

"Spearings was like Woolworths, you could buy paint, Mr Spearing sold the paint, that was down one side of the shop, then on the other side there was all sorts of things - haberdashery, sweets, cigarettes, biscuits, groceries and she had a bacon slicer. You went there for a card of elastic to mend your knickers, and bias binding for making your aprons, and darning wool and ribbons. Mr Spearing was out the back, he did carpentry, he did a lot of work in the church, he was always up there mending and he did all sorts of odd jobs."
Margaret Porter (née Webb)

Aerial view of Laburnum House showing Hunts shop and post box (left), Hillborne and Spearings shop (right)

Poole Farm, abattoir and butcher, c1900

Harold Webb with horse at Fir Tree Farm Henley, where his mother and stepfather (Sarah and John Gooding) ran a shop, c1907

"I remember the butchers shop where Poole Farm is, I remember the blood-stained water running from the slaughterhouse into the pool, a sort of large ditch which was there by the road, it's filled in now. The door gave onto the road, it would be open, we couldn't see the slaughterhouse inside, the floor was scrubbed and this river of red water flowed out and when we walked to school we had to step over it. I don't remember it ever smelling. I remember we took our cattle there to be slaughtered, and he may probably have had his own cattle too - butchers in those days were farmer butchers. I remember he was very particular about his beef. It was all so local, you'd know whose bullock it was. People would say, 'Oh, such and such a farmer just had his bullock killed today, and we'd say, 'Well we'd better go and buy a joint'. You knew whose meat it was, you'd watched it in the field, you knew the farmer." Peggy Coombes (née Vigar)

"There was a bakery just past the school, down the dip and there was a butchers shop on the left, Poole Farm. There was the baker's van that came round. There weren't many cars. You were rich if you had a bicycle!" Linda Lavis (née Gould)

"Mr Lockyer was the baker, where the Agricentre is now. I used to grease all the tins. Mr Lockyer would pass bits of dough and I would knead it and put it in the tins to prove. He made cakes, lardy cakes, fruit cakes, always the same things. I used to help Mrs Lockyer with the washing. Her wash house was across the yard from the big house. She was so particular about rinsing. I used to have to rinse and rinse again in cold water. Mrs Lockyer used to do the pastry in the bakehouse. I can see her now coming across with her bowl and flour to make pastry in the bakehouse. She was so particular and didn't like mess in her house. She used to make tarts." Edna Webb (née Sherrin)

"There were shops in Henley over the years, but there was only ever one at a time. Before the war my Aunt Mary and Percy Williams had a shop at Fir Tree Farm, they were farmers there but they also sold general things, butter, sugar, tea. Nobody had cars then. After the war, Mrs Sheppard at Pettys Cottage sold sweets, and then after that Charlie and Cissy Webb did at the bottom of Stout." Ethel Webb

"Between the wars, we used to get round on our bikes or by pony and trap. We didn't go far, just to market. There was no need. Everything came to us - a draper would come from Taunton, and grocers, the ironmonger, two or three bakers and a butcher - Butcher Sherrin. Mr Vickery came with a horse and cart with paraffin and candles and all sorts, and men with suitcases came selling things. Later, Mr Clark from Taunton came in a car with clothes, you'd order it and he'd bring it on, we had Clark' shoes, Crockers used to come round with shoes and they'd take shoes to repair, they'd take them on a Tuesday and bring them back Fridays. There were coal lorries, and there was a turf man who came selling peat, Mr Curtis brought oil and china and hardware and he'd buy rabbit skins off you for a halfpenny, Mr Vickery did too." Ethel Webb

"Mr Kick, he had a little shop in Drayton before the war, and a little van came round with an open door at the back and you stepped up into the van and gave your order. The only thing I believe you had to go to town for, the ladies had to go for a hat now and again." Guy Tapscott

"We did go to Langport shopping, but people came round to us. There was an agent for the Langport Stores, and she'd cycle out to us on her bicycle, collect orders and then later in the week they'd deliver our order. And Mr Pocock, he had a van and sold everything – paraffin, toilet rolls, brushes, pots, pans… It was an open lorry with all the pots and pans hanging and clanking. He had anything you needed. He'd call once a week. After the war all that finished, cars came and people didn't need deliveries." Peggy Coombes (née Vigar)

"We grew up in High Ham in the 1940s, 50s and early 60s. Fishy Cooper, who was the man from the wet fish shop in Somerton, where the fish and chip shop is now, he came round in a van selling his fish. Mr Watts came round with glass batteries for the radio. They were very heavy; I remember him carrying them up the garden path. He gave a new one for the radio and took the old one away to top up. Maisey's Bakery van came round too, although in the old days there was a bakery in the village. I remember the hot cross buns before Easter, but only on one day of the year, so that was a special treat." [1] Anna McCallion and Mary Ann Miller

Maisey's bread van, Dennis Legg the driver [1]

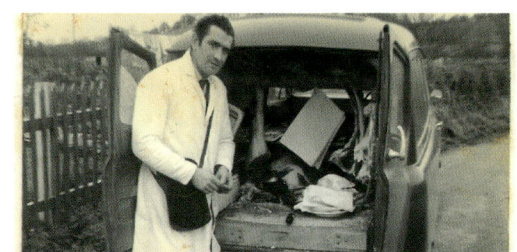

Sid Ackerman, the driver for Mrs Widdicombe who had the butcher's shop in Somerton late 1950s [1]

The Nurse and Dentist

"The Sherrin family lived at Gawlers Farm and my grandmother, Agnes Windsor, lived at the top of the hill. In February 1931 Mrs Sherrin went into labour in the middle of the night. Her husband ran up the hill and woke my grandmother up and then he went off to harness his pony and trap to ride to Huish to fetch the midwife. My grandmother went down to help and ended up delivering the baby herself. By the time Mr Sherrin got back with the midwife the baby was dry and dressed. That baby was Ned Sherrin who became well known in radio and television." Peggy Coombes (née Vigar)

"I remember Nurse Gooding's Austin 7. I left the village when I got married but my husband was in the Air Force and I came back to Mother in 1940 to have my baby. Nurse Gooding drove me to Taunton Hospital. It was probably in that car in the photograph."
(See page 108 for photo of car) Freda Hayes (née Cullen)

"In the 1950s Nurse Gooding lived alone in one of the cottages which are no longer there, near the pub. The house was full of chickens and she used to sit in her armchair nursing one or two. She had a little driveway where she sold petrol and when they dug up the road to put the water in they put planks over the trench so she could drive in. Sometimes when the locals left the pub at night they'd remove the planks and when she drove her car out she ended up with her wheels in the trench!" Bill Westcott

"Before the National Health a lot of families belonged to the Langport Nursing Association. Mrs Carne-Hill was the president. My mother was one of the collectors and I used to go with her, and Mrs Davis was another one. If you belonged you paid five shillings a year for a nursing facility for the family. A lot of the people paid quarterly, one shilling and threepence. They would say, 'Do come in and have a cup of tea while you are here'. There would be no sign of the money until you'd been there some time. Then it was, 'I'd better find you the money as I put it back 'cos I knew you were coming'. The families could have the District Nurse. The last one was Nurse Hill and she had a car. She delivered babies. When Mother had a baby the nurse would call in every morning, and wash the baby and the mother, and make sure the baby was putting on weight." Joy Vigar (née Sherrin)

"Charlie Keevil at Low Ham was a blacksmith. You paid sixpence to have a tooth drawn and an extra tuppence for his daughter to hold your head! That was going back to before the war." Ethel Webb

"They had the school dentist who used to come occasionally. He had a treadle drill, he filled one of my teeth with a treadle which I remember, that really did hurt." Brian Hill

The Kings Head

"My grandmother, Elizabeth Ann, and her first husband, took over the Kings Head before the First World War. Her husband, Edward Gould, died in 1913, aged 36. He was a blacksmith and had a smithy at the pub. They had three daughters, Louisa, Vera and Lesley. After her husband died my grandmother advertised for another blacksmith to continue the business. Luke Inder replied and soon after my gran married him and they had a son, Harry, born in 1915. Sadly my grandfather died in 1930, aged 48. My gran went on running the pub. They kept a few cows as well to produce milk for extra income." Sheila Jewell (née Inder)

Elizabeth and Luke Inder with baby Harry, 1915

Elizabeth Inder, landlady of the Kings Head, High Ham, standing outside the pub with her daughter and Uncle Harry Woodman, c1920

Harry Inder, The Kings Head, High Ham, c1920. The cottages on the right were demolished in the 1960s and the orchard on the left is now houses.

Ham Court Shakespearian actors at the pub, 1920s-30s

"I remember the Kings Head pub in the late 1940s, early 50s, that's when Bob and Mary Crossman and their son had it. The gypsies used to come and camp in the orchard opposite. One other chap I remember coming was a small chap who had a large shire stallion and he'd take it round all the farms. I remember seeing him tie it up outside the pub. It was busy. In those days there weren't many cars and life gyrated round the church and the pub. I stayed there when I first came to the village. It was a good old country pub." Bill Westcott

"Mum and Dad, Maisie and Walt Brown, bought the pub from the brewery, Watneys, about 1956. It had originally been a cider house, but it was already selling ale when they bought it. I was born there. It was a pretty lively place. Everybody knew it as Maisies."
Pete Brown

Walt and Maisie Brown, landlord and landlady of the Kings Head from 1956.

"I was on my way up to Ham pub and cut through by what is now Long Street Cottage, when I came across my Uncle Den lying spreadeagled in the snow on the ground. He was on his way back home from the pub. I managed to rouse him and asked what he was going to do, he brushed himself down and said, 'I think I'll lie down again and wait for the spring'. It was November!
There were lots of other drinking places, cider drinking - Harold Webb's at Poplar Farm, Wilkins' at Walnut Tree Farm, Hacky Crossman's, Harry Inder's at Gawler's Farm... I remember once at Harry Webb's, I got on my motorbike to go home, rather the worse for wear - locally known as Somerset flu! My bike had a puncture on the front tyre, so I thought I better drive quickly before it was completely flat. I drove through the open door of the shed at home, straight through and out the other end. I ended up on the ground with the exhaust against my calves, burning a hole through my leg. I couldn't stop laughing - until the next day!" Brian Hill

"My dad, Harry Inder, grew up in the King's Head and my brother, Charlie, was born there. Then he came here to Gawlers Farm around 1940 and me and my sister were born here. He made cider and everybody walking up the hill would be asked 'Do you want a drop of cider?' There were lots of cider-makers, and if you didn't want a drink of their cider, they'd want to know what was wrong with it! There were such characters here - you'll never see the likes of it again. Dad used to have the gypsies here to pick beans and peas. We had all the horse-drawn caravans here, fifteen or more and there would be 20 or 30 horses. The kids went to school with us. The gypsies would come in the spring, stay for the summer, then go to Kent hop-picking. It was always lively here on a Saturday night. It was great fun, I loved it all."
Les Inder

"I first went into the pub when I was a teenager, learning to ring the bells, in the late 1950s. The beer used to be kept behind the bar in wooden barrels, Ushers Triple X, and in warm weather Walt would keep the beer cool with wet towels on the barrels. The pub was good, Maisie was a character and she kept the place in order. There were lots of pea pickers came, they had the original canvas wagons and we often went up to where they were camped and they'd have a camp fire and we'd have a great time with them." Tony Cullen

Queuing for the Doctor's surgery in the Kings Head, 1960s

"In the 1960s the doctor's surgery was held in the pub, Wednesday afternoon, two o'clock, Doctor Henderson. There was a room with a couch in it. You went in through the door on the left, it's all changed now. You went into the passageway to wait. We all knew each other - there wasn't much we didn't know about each other in those days, it was village life." Sheila Jewell (née Inder)

The Village Policeman

"The School House was a Police Station in my time, I certainly remember it as a Police Station up to the late 1920s. PC Pitman lived there with his wife and children. There was very little crime. Riding a bicycle without lights was the most pernicious. I suppose we were a very orderly lot, if you misbehaved it went round the village like wildfire and then there was a timely word in someone's ear, that was enough."
Freda Hayes (née Cullen)

"I remember once in the 1920s or 30s, when the policeman was drunk, as drunk as he could be, and he said to my mother's brother, 'Could you do my round tonight, got to go round High Ham and Low Ham, I can't go', he was drunk. He said to my mother's brother, 'Here have my uniform', and so my mother's brother did, and nobody knew, he went all round, and nobody ever knew." Linda Lavis (née Gould)

c1900 The Old School House, High Ham, built in 1598 by the Rector, Adrien Schael. During the early years of the 20th century there was a Reading Room on the ground floor where daily papers were available. From 1915–1932 it was occupied by various village policemen. The village pump is on the verge on the right and the wall behind was a noticeboard. The pump was used until water was piped into the village in the 1950s. It was removed some time in the early 1960s.

"I remember sometimes the policemen used to come into the pub and have a quiet drink in the snug and Walt would say, 'Keep it down lads, the coppers are in'. We used to have two coppers from Langport, they came out pretty regularly, and often you'd see a little glow outside Hunts' shop, and it would be one of the policemen having a fag, and he'd say, 'You haven't seen me!'"
Tony Cullen

PC Standen [2]

"In the late 1950s the police would come round on Thursdays to check the villages. The policeman would come on his bicycle to Low Ham and ring from the phone box at Low Ham to check in, and then cycle to High Ham to use the public call box outside Mrs Hunt's. We would stuff bangers, rockets and suchlike into our bicycle pumps, pump them up, light the fuse and shoot them across The Green as the policeman arrived. We would run off and hide in the grounds of the Rectory which was becoming derelict by then. The police used to go up to the pub and do a quick look on all the kids to make sure they weren't drinking. Pearcy (Mr Pearce the policeman) would come on a Velocette and when he arrived somebody would say they were going to the loo, but they would go and swap over the plug leads on the bike. It would go pop and bang all over the place. He got used to this being done, but once when he came we hadn't done anything, but he swapped over the leads himself before setting off anyway and it banged loudly everywhere." Brian Hill

Transport

"Mostly it was 'shank's pony' - we used to walk everywhere!"
Ron Tapscott

The Pony and Trap

Gordon and Brian Vigar with Gran Vigar and their mother, Gwen, in their governess car with Jimmy, the pony, Bridge Farm, Henley, 1927-8

"We had a trap horse, a horse that used to go in a governess car. Even when we got a motor car in about 1929 (a Morris Cowley, with steps up the side and a horn) I don't remember ever going shopping in the car before the war, only the pony and trap. After the war, from 1945 onwards, that's when cars came and the ponies and traps stopped."
Peggy Coombes (née Vigar)

"I went to school at four years old, about 1922. We all walked up but sometimes Father used to put us in the horse and trap and take us through the floods till we got to the hill and then we had to run up the hill to school. I always had friends to walk with. Oh, my parents never came with me, I don't think they ever went to school."
Linda Lavis (née Gould)

"There were several different types of horse drawn vehicles. The governess car had a step at the back and a door and seats both sides, this was usually varnished, cheerful-looking. It was for ladies and children. The putt had a shaft with tipping mechanism. It would be used for mangles, for example. They were hand-picked and taken to a big grave and tipped into it and covered over for winter feed for the animals. There was also a little spring wagon, a small wagon for farm work, light work, a run-around vehicle used on the farm. Then there was the cart or trap, sometimes called a float. It was pulled by a horse with shafts, it had a seat for the driver and people would take it down to the moors milking and bring the churns back in it. Then there was the gig, this was more posh, used if the farmer was going to town, to the bank for example. They were all made by local carpenters and they were all individual." Peggy Coombes (née Vigar)

Robert Charles Davis with son Dennis, Ham Court, c1935. *"I remember that day very well, we were going to the mill at Othery to get oats for the horse, they ground them there and we came back with big sacks."* Dennis Davis

The Bicycle

Aunt Ness Lloyd [1], c1910

"We might have to walk to Langport to do our shopping, Mother used to say, 'Don't talk to nobody on the way'. I were around 13 or 14 perhaps, about 1930. We didn't know anything different. I didn't have a bicycle till about 1935, I were 18, couldn't afford one before. It were a lot of money, five pounds it was." Linda Lavis (née Gould)

"I was a keen cyclist. I cycled down to the Quantocks to see my grandparents on my own when I was about eleven, about 1940, which was quite something - near Bagborough, about 30 miles. I cycled to school every day, to Huish, there was half a dozen of us at least. I went to Huish when I was eleven and stayed till I was 14 and started working. You had to have a bicycle to go to Huish, the vast majority stayed at High Ham. It was two or three years after the end of the war probably before they started transporting children from this village to Huish." Dennis Davis

"We used to cycle everywhere, Shirley and I cycled to Wells Cathedral one day, all the way from Low Ham. It was somewhere we wanted to go. Of course the roads weren't like they are today. We must have been 12 or 13, about 1952. We took a picnic and when we got there we sat and watched the swans ring the bell. We left our bikes propped up against a tree, of course you wouldn't do that today, and to think of doing that now with all the traffic… and we used to cycle to dances in Moorlinch and Aller. We'd come back in the dark up Turn Hill.
Then later when I was 15 I started work at Clarks in Street. I had to walk or cycle from High Ham to White Hill, the other end of Wearne, where the road goes to Aller and Langport. On the fork there was a little tin shed and the army used to let us put our bicycles there. Walt Brown lived next to me and we used to cycle together. I can remember vividly having to walk from High Ham because we couldn't cycle when the snow was so deep and thick. They only cleared the main road, not the side roads." Gwen Chubb (née Bown)

"When we went to secondary school we still had to get up to The Green at High Ham. The bus didn't come down to Henley. We had to push our bikes up the hill and leave them somewhere on The Green. That was until I was 15, 1958, we still didn't have the school bus down Henley." Tony Meaker

"In the late 1950s John Loader, Tony Meaker and me, we'd plan to go to the pictures in Street and that night we'd meet up in High Ham on our bikes and then we'd charge down the hill shouting and hollering as loud as we could so our mates in Henley could hear us, and then when they heard us they would start pedalling and come out on the road at the bottom, and we'd all shout loudly so we knew whether they were in front or behind and we'd catch each other up." Les Inder

John Wheadon and Heather Humphries, 1951

Clockwise from top left:
William Henry Fouracre outside his shop on Picts Hill, 1930s. His trade card describes him as *'Cycle Agent and Antiques Dealer. Agent for BSA, Humber, James, Royal Enfield, Olympic, Rovers'*. He also repaired cycles and sold petrol in cans;

Ham Court, possibly celebration of King George V1 Coronation, 1938;

Gares Cottages, Low Ham, c1950. Left to right: Nora Ford, Phil Scriven, Arthur Scriven, Fred Ford, Maureen Scriven, Sheila Scriven, Henry Ford, Phyllis Hurd, Andy Ford and Vera Ford;

King George V Silver Jubilee Celebrations, Ham Court, 10 May 1935. Left to right foreground: Rev EBA Hughes, Robert Charles Davis, George Sherrin;

Rev EBA Hughes with his family at the Rectory, High Ham, on 13 August 1930, the day of his daughter Philothea's marriage to John Robinson

Early Cars

Mrs Carne-Hill's car. Chauffeur Robert Charles Davis with Mrs Catherine Watts and daughter, 1920s

"This was the last car Mrs Carne-Hill had, a 1938 Ford 10. When she died in 1943 she left it in her will to my father." Dennis Davis

"There was a time when Mrs Carne-Hill left her car parked at the top of Langport Hill, by the surgery, where the Grammar School was, and she didn't put the brake on properly and it just ran down the hill, narrowly missing Mrs Coombes and her son David. It smashed into the shop window at the bottom (where Lafleure is now) and Mrs Carne-Hill said, 'Well they needed a new shop window!'. That would have been in the 1930s."
Dennis Davis

"In High Ham Orland Lavis and the Hunts had the shops. They had cars, and Mrs Carne-Hill. Our Aunt Molly was the only one who had a car in Henley. This was before the war. The car was only used to take people to the doctors or to the hospital or market then. It wasn't for the seaside or enjoying yourself. It was for emergencies or work." Ethel Webb

Trojan three-wheeler at Fir Tree Farm, Henley (where there was a shop earlier, see photo, page 99)

"There were two hand pumps for petrol in the village in Ham - one where the village baker was, opposite Poole Farm, and the other Nurse Gooding had, she was the village nurse. She had a car quite early on and then she got a petrol pump where she lived, she sold petrol when she retired, there was a pump there, where St. Andrews Close is now, near the pub." Ron Tapscott

"During the war, I was about 17, I applied for a driving licence, and because it was in the war there was a question about what you were prepared to drive and I said I was willing to drive an ambulance if needs be, so I got a licence straightaway, and I could drive anything, I could have driven articulated lorries, tanks, lots of things! I never did drive an ambulance. I never did have to take a test and I had my licence from that time." Peggy Coombes (née Vigar)

High Ham, 1920s. Nurse Gooding's house (on left) and her car.

Doris Hill who escaped London with her baby daughter, Pam, in the first years of the Second World War and stayed at Hillside Cottage, High Ham.

"There were a few cars in the war but you had to have a special permit to get one. Father did because he had to take calves to market. He took them with a pony but then the market closed in Langport and he had to take them to Bridgwater. He got permission to have a car then, it was too far for the pony. But not many people had cars."
Ron Tapscott

"Vic Dyer used to mend cars and punctures, Bill Baker was where the Agricentre is, he had three or four cattle lorries and he sold petrol. I remember in the early 1960s you could fill up the pick-up truck for £1. Petrol was four shillings a gallon, that's 20 pence in today's money."
Tony Meaker

"In the 1950s my husband rented a big shed behind the pub to work in. Then later he applied for permission to build the garage, that's how the garage came to be built, in the 1960s. Vic sold petrol and repaired cars. He liked his work, but he wasn't too keen on the paperwork. I did all the bills and that side of the business. Apart from going to the pub, he was in the garage. He died in 1992." Una Dyer

Roadworks

Local stone breakers, c1914

Road repairs with steam roller at junction of main road to High Ham and turning to Wearne, c1914

"In the photo Will Sherrin is on the far left and Jim Hill is there with his horse on the far right. It was before the war. Jim went to the war, and Will. Will's brother Sid was killed, but Will came back. The picture of the stone breakers is probably about the same time. The stones came from Long Sutton quarry probably. Our father always told us that a couple of chaps would sit on the side of the road cracking stones, then when they'd cracked them they'd 'yard them up', and they got paid by the yard." Ron Tapscott

Steam roller at Henley Corner Farm, c1920. Picture includes: Roy Cox (lived at Henley Corner Farm), Frank Gover and Charlie Cox

"There was a large green on the corner outside Henley Corner Farm, it was still there after I left school in the mid-1930s, then the road got widened and so did the drove and then one day the tarmac just covered it over. It was always the site of a great bonfire on Guy Fawkes night, but after that we didn't have the bonfire any more.
For road scraping they had a little machine on two wheels and they could push it down, bear down on it, and then pull it back and scrape the mud off the road, it was very thick the mud then, this was before tarmac. In the 1920s, when I went to school there was only tarmac on the main road through High Ham, that was the only road where we could play tops." Ron Tapscott

Lil, Den and Arthur Scriven, 1950s

"This photo was taken by Honeysuckle Cottage in Low Ham, with the Council-owned steam roller in the background by The Pound. When I was a boy we still called it The Pound even though it wasn't used as one anymore. The steam roller was driven by Ted Castle and at the end of the day he used to cycle home, he'd have his bicycle strapped to the roller during the day. Ted Castle even drove that steam roller down Turn Hill!" Brian Hill

Trains and Buses

Village outing to Cheddar, c1930. Gwen Vigar next to coach driver with her children Peggy and Henry, and Granny and Grandpa Windsor behind.

"My mother's sister lived at Washfield, outside Tiverton. My mum used to visit her and when she did she'd get up early, cycle into Langport, catch a train to Taunton from the station in Langport,[3] change at Taunton, and then get the train to Cove Station, a single track line, then she walked to her sister's farm and she'd be there by 11. Then in the evening she'd walk back to the station, get the train to Taunton, change, get to Langport Station and cycle home and she'd be home by 10 o'clock. That's something you can't imagine today!"
Peggy Coombes (née Vigar)

"We used to get the train at Langport Station,[3] we called it the 'bucket'. It was one big coach with seats all down through. The station went in 1964.
Sandfords ran a bus on Wednesdays before the war, it stopped in Henley and went to Bridgwater. Later there was a National bus on Saturdays to Bridgwater and back. We went to market sometimes."
Ethel Webb

"It was a farming village. The big revolution was, I suppose, at the end of the war when suddenly Clarks started employing a lot more labour locally and they ran a coach from Langport to Street. There was a deuce of a lot of people employed by Clarks then."
Dennis Davis

Motorbikes and Moving House

Low Ham. From left: Fred and Vera Ford, Arthur Scriven and Rita Ford, Ted Ceaser and Alma Ford, 1951

"I got my first motorbike in 1958, it was a Scott and it cost £12.50. We could afford bikes, whereas we couldn't afford cars. There was a group of us, we used to do things together, we'd all go to Taunton, or we'd all go up to Turn Hill and talk. We had a lot of fun. We used to help each other with the mechanics." Pete Rossiter

Turn Hill, 1958. From left: Cliff Crossman, Mike Sherrin, Ron Wheadon, Geoff Hollard, Len Cox, Pete Rossiter, Tom Hodge and Jimmy Upham (boy)

The Ford family moving to Stembridge Lea, Low Ham, 5 August 1962

Low Ham Sports Day, c1965

One of the last working horses in Henley digging out a rotten bridge, Straight Drove, Somerton Moor, 1963. Left to right: Len Cox digging, Charlie Webb and Jack Cox (Len's Dad) watching.

"We used to walk everywhere, or cycle. You could walk down Alabaster Lane (that's at the end of Fountain and it's called Alabaster because there's alabaster there), you could walk right down to Wilkins, and then turn left and go out to the end at Heavens Gate, that was Travis Farm then. This was in the 1950s. They were wonderful days, there was none of this 'health and safety' then. There was so much freedom - but if you stepped out of line you got punished. We could leave home all day and our parents were never worried. We used to look for birds' nests or we used to go down to Aller Milk Factory where they pumped effluent onto the Moors, it used to stink a bit, and was very squelchy, but it was fantastic because it used to breed lots of grass snakes. Or we used to go out with guns shooting pigeons and rabbits, we were probably about 11 or 12 or 13, and we used to trap rabbits - we used to walk miles. You used to be able to come from Langport and the hedges all the way used to be full of the yellowhammers, packed out, and skylarks in the fields - and we used to lie on our backs and if you were lucky you'd see them and you'd hear them right up in the sky - and green plovers, we used to call them peewits, and we used to go down across the moors and watch the reed buntings. There used to be lots of large elms and quite a few of the lads used to climb right to the top of the elms and collect the eggs from rooks' nests and have egg fights up there. We used to go off all day. We never took anything to eat with us. Our mothers would say, 'Be back for lunch' - but we never were, we were never hungry. If there were orchards we'd eat the apples - Bramleys, Morgan Sweets. We never thought about food, it never went through your mind, and we'd not come back home till teatime."

Tony Cullen

Footnotes

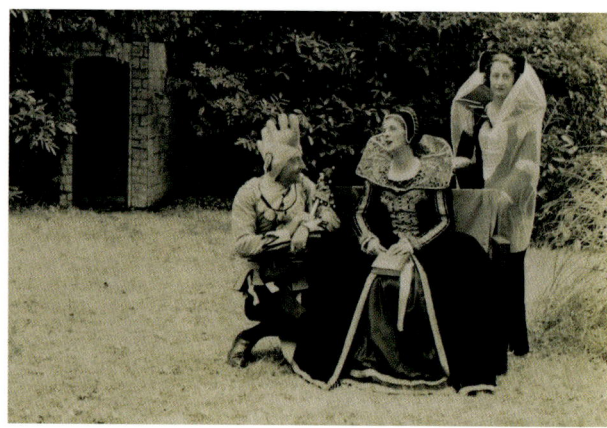

FOREWORD
1. Manor Farm, High Ham (Somerset Heritage Service Ref: A/CLV\M\1740).

THE TURN OF THE CENTURY
1. The Sherrin family: see page 12 The War Years 1914-1918 and footnote 2 below.

THE WAR YEARS 1914-18
1. Men who joined the West Somerset Yeomanry from the Langport area were in C Squadron of the WSY. The WSY (part of the Territorial Force) was a mounted territorial cavalry unit formed of volunteers and was nearly at full strength when war broke out on 4 August 1914. The volunteer soldiers in the WSY were called up immediately.
2. Sherrin family photographs and wartime letters were rescued by neighbour Ron Tapscott from a bonfire at Yew Tree Farm after the last surviving brother, Percy Sherrin, died in the 1980s. None of the Sherrin boys married or had children. (Somerset Heritage Service Ref: A\DPY/3).
3. The British Legion Book of Remembrance, on public view in The Church of St. Andrew, High Ham, lists 118 men from High Ham Parish who fought in the First World War, highlighting in red 19 men who did not return: Bryson Bellot, Victor Chapple, Francis Cox, Guy Crossman, Henry Cullen, Edward Fisher, Charles Frith, Percy Garland, Maurice Lloyd, Champion Mead, James Mead, Albert Open, Charles Rood, Walter Townsend, Sidney Sherrin, Anthony Thyer, Henry Thyer, Augustus Wilkins and Reginald Woodman.
4. Somerset Heritage Service Ref: A\CLV/1740.
5. There are six memorials in High Ham: 1. Marble Tablet (Church), erected 1921, lists 18 men from the parish who died. 2. Calvary (Churchyard) erected by the brother of Lt. Guy Crossman. 3. Memorial tablet erected by Mr and Mrs Mead in the Church to their only two children who died within a week of each other. 4. British Legion Book of Remembrance. 5. Land at Turn Hill was presented to the National Trust by Hugh and Beatrice Bellot in memory of their son. There is a hamstone plaque on the stone wall at the entrance to the land. 6. High Ham Memorial Hall (see below).
6. The Village Memorial Hall was designed by Philip Tilden (1887-1956) who made his reputation working on commissions from clients that included Winston Churchill, David Lloyd George and Lady Ottoline Morrell. Tilden gave his professional services free to High Ham as a tribute to Lt. Bryson Bellot. The ambition for the High Ham Memorial Hall was to form "...a link between them (the 19 men who died) and the living, something making for social betterment, something giving an uplift to village life, something which would make the village a better and brighter place in which to dwell." Dr HHL Bellot.

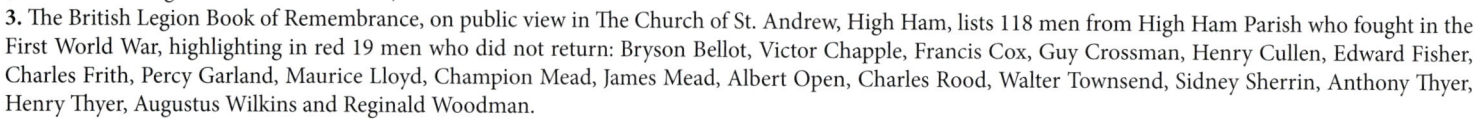

SHAKESPEARE AT THE COURT
1. Mrs Carne-Hill (1861-1943) raised money for the Nursing Association funds from the Shakespeare productions.

THE WAR YEARS 1939-45
1. Ronald Gray (1868-1951). Figure and landscape painter in oil and watercolour. Friend and follower of Steer. Studied at the Westminster School of Art and the Académie Julian, Paris. Visited America in 1908, 1909 and 1910. Member of the NEAC. Exhibited at the Royal Academy and at the Paris Salon (Silver Medal); one-man exhibition at the Goupil Gallery 1923.
2. The bombed house is now known as Shorelands, Low Ham.
3. The Golf Links is the local name for the land at the top of Hext Hill (where the annual Steam Rally is held today). It was the Mid-Somerset Golf Club, a nine-hole golf course, founded in 1894. The entry fee was 1 guinea, subs 1 guinea, visitors' fees 1 shilling and sixpence a day, five shillings a week and 10 shillings a month. Sunday play was not allowed. It was still there in the late 1930s and the last mention is 1947. *"It was a pukka golf course, nicely mown, they had a club house."* Dulcie Davis.
4. Stanley Cornwell Lewis MBE (1905-2009) studied at Newport School of Art and Royal College of Art. In 1937 his painting 'Welsh Molecatcher' was voted the most popular picture in the Royal Academy Summer Exhibition (purchased by Newport Museum and Art Gallery). In 1941 he joined army training at Rhyl, North Wales, and was posted to the 66th Searchlight Regiment, part of the Somerset Gloucester Regiment. He was commissioned to paint 'Morning Maintenance on a Searchlight Site' in 1943. This painting, made at Low Ham, has been lost. Stanley was then transferred to Fleet Air Arm, Yeovil, and commissioned to paint 'The Attack on the Tirpitz'. He was Principal of Carmarthen School of Art until 1968 and worked as professional artist and illustrator throughout his life. Liss Fine Art mounted a retrospective in 2010. The fully illustrated book 'Stanley Lewis' is available from his daughter, Jennifer Heywood (jenheywood45@hotmail.co.uk) who continues to work on her father's war archives.

5. The Langport Union Workhouse was erected in 1837-9 at Picts Hill, Langport. It was based on Sampson Kempthorne's model hexagonal plan published by the Poor Law Commissioners in 1835. It was a workhouse until c1931. During the Second World War the building was used as military detention centre. After the war it was used as a poultry and egg packing facility by the Prideaux family (farmers at Bowdens). The buildings were later left derelict. They were demolished and developed as Hamdown Court in 2003.

6. *"With the threat of invasion imminent in the summer of 1940, High Ham Home Guard kept a nighttime vigil over the countryside looking towards Pitney from a hut erected close to High Ham Windmill. Turn Hill was also used as an observation point. One of the duties of Long Sutton Platoon, in conjunction with Langport and High Ham Home Guards, was to guard the western portal of the Somerton Tunnel and ventilation shaft on Somerton Hill. For the convenience of the guards, huts were erected at both spots. For carrying out this duty the men were paid two shillings (ten pence) a night which could last up to ten hours. During the day a detachment of the Coldstream Guards protected the tunnel. No sleeping in wooden huts for them, they were billeted at the Devonshire Arms (Long Sutton)."* (From 'The Somerset Home Guard, a pictorial roll call' by Jeffrey Wilson, pub. Millstream Books Isbn 0948975717).

7. The Gold Flake sign outside Gares Cottage where Amy Ford lived with her children is in the permanent collection of the Somerset Heritage Service.

8. Wimsheet: a large piece of sail cloth. The word comes from 'winnowing sheet', used to create a current of air to separate edible grain from chaff.

The Langport Union Workhouse

HIGH DAYS AND HOLIDAYS

1. Poem from 'Tommy Nutty's Feast Day' by W. Cook.
2. The Women's Benefit Society seems to have been active in the 1890s up until about 1910. The Headmaster noted in the High Ham School Log Book (Somerset Heritage Service Ref: A/BXW/2/1) when the school closed each year for the Women's Benefit Society Anniversary in June (last date noted 24 June 1910).
3. From the late 18th century the term Friendly Society (often called a Club) describes a group of people who formed an organisation and agreed to make regular contributions of money for distribution to members at times of ill health, old age and to pay funeral costs. In the parish of High Ham there were three societies: the Women's Benefit Society (see above), the Kings Head Club (dates unknown) and the School House Club (1852 - 1931). Each Friendly Society had its Club Day and Parade (usually May/June). Most Friendly Societies faded out with the coming of the state pension and the National Health Service.
4. The stave heads illustrated, also known as pole heads/staff heads, are from two of High Ham's clubs. The stave with the crown is possibly from the Kings Head Club, (permanent collection of the Museum of Rural Life, Reading Ref: 55/1015). The other stave could be from one of the other High Ham clubs (permanent collection Somerset Heritage Service).
5. Bibby and Sons were cattle feed suppliers based in Bridgwater and offered outings to local farmers who were their customers.
6. Extract from Article MT086 Musical Traditions No 2, 'Mrs Amy Ford of Low Ham Somerset – song learning in a family tradition' by Bob and Jacqueline Patten. (Amy Ford 1905-1983).
7. This photograph of Harvest Festival at Low Ham Chapel (preacher unknown) came from Sandra Hayes via the High Ham Parish Community Project website. Sandra bought a collection of photographs and postcards in a car boot sale. The postcards, dated between 1900 and 1910, were addressed to Mrs Lloyd, Fir Tree Farm, Low Ham. Sandra contacted the High Ham Parish Community Project and sent copies of the photographs.

LIFE AT SCHOOL

1. Extracts are taken from the High Ham School Log Books (Somerset Heritage Service Ref: A\BXW/2/1). Headteachers were required to keep a daily record of occurrences in the life of the school. Entries included: information about pupil attendance and factors which affected attendance, such as extreme weather, local epidemics or children helping with the harvest; information about teaching staff; the visits of inspectors; timetables and the subjects taught; building problems; cases of bad behaviour; celebratory events and any other significant incidents. During the Second World War, they also included information about evacuees. The headteacher had to make an entry in the log book at least once a week. It was important to keep the log book up to date and accurate as the School Inspector would check them on every visit.
2. Postcard of the School, High Ham in the 1930s. The original Victorian school was built in the 1860s with the first entry in the school log book on the 4 April 1864. This building was demolished in 1987 and the new school was officially opened 20 October 1988.
3. One of the Sherrin family's photographs (see 'The War Years 1914-1918' footnote 2).
4. Extracts from High Ham Log Books noted by Jane Lines. Jane was an amateur local historian documenting life in the parish. She was a frequent visitor to the Somerset Record Office (now Somerset Heritage Centre). She recorded everything of interest in a large diary.
5. 'The Big School' is the local colloquial term for the Secondary school. After Second World War most pupils went to Huish Episcopi Secondary School (now Huish Academy) at 11, when school transport was laid on. Previously they had stayed at High Ham School until they were 14. Most of those who passed their 11+ went to the Grammar Schools in Taunton, Bridgwater or Street.

FARMING

Before the First World War, most of the land was owned by one of two large estates. This land was farmed by tenant farmers and agricultural labourers employed by them. After the war the land and farmyards were sold off in small blocks enabling many to buy a few acres. By 1939 there were over 60 farms/smallholdings in High Ham Parish, most of which were under 50 acres.

1. The Shire stallion described by Peggy Coombes would have come from The Yeovil Shire Horse Society. In their brochure for the 1933 season the stallion is Pinchbeck Friar Champion 40509, foaled 1927. It lists his prestigious pedigree and notes that Pinchbeck is 'a *big upstanding horse, with good wearing limbs and the best of feet and joints...*' The stallion has a weekly route - Saturday being Henley, High and Low Ham, Long Sutton (stands at Messrs. Parsons & Sons, Long Sutton Saturday till Monday). The fee was £2 10s (£2.50). The groom's fee was three shillings (15p) to be paid to the groom at first time of service.

2. The strakes fixed to the wheel were an accessory fitted to the rear wheels of tractors to obtain more traction when ploughing. They were effective but noisy in use. They were used prior to the introduction of four-wheel drive tractors.

3. Pitney Harbour was a sheep wash. It was near Joe Meaker's mangold cutting barn, Pitney. There was a pipe which the stream ran through all the time. When they needed to wash the sheep prior to shearing, they put a board across the end of the pipe to stop the water escaping. This filled up the 'harbour' and the sheep were hunted through the deep water. There was a second pipe higher up that took the overflow.

4. The photographs of the cheese presses have been taken from '1969 Past in the Present', compiled by Mrs Williams of Keepers Cottage, Low Ham, as an entry in a WI County Competition in 1969. It won a Gold Star.

5. Ethel Webb (daughter of Ada Vigar and Harold Webb) grew up in Henley and was a cheesemaker from 1940 to 1970, first for Aunty Molly (Mary Jane Tapscott) at Henley Farm, then at Cannington, Chewton Mendip and Wells. She describes making cheddar cheese at Henley Farm in 1940: "*The first thing I'd do in the morning was to light the boiler to heat the night's milk in the cheese vat. I'd add the starter when the temperature was right. That would stay until the morning milk was added. Then I'd bring the temperature up to 85ºF. It had to be the right acidity too. We had a pipette, caustic soda and 'phenophane' – 3 drops of that and the sample would turn pink if it was right. The rennet would go in next and be left for about 40 minutes till it had gone like junket. Then I'd cut it with a curd knife, bring the temperature up to 100ºF and stir and rake it for 2 hours. I let the curd settle then put my hands right down in to the whey, push the curds to one end of the vat and let the whey drain away and be fed to the pigs. The curd was cut into blocks and put on the cooler and turned every 20 minutes, putting dry cloths in between the curd blocks every time. When they were fully ripe and the acidity okay, I put them in a curd mill, turn it by hand, mix in salt, put them in moulds, turn and press them. Next day they were tipped out, hot water poured over, clean dry cloths wrapped round and back in to the press. Next day lard was put on them and clean muslin. The next day I tipped them out and put a sort of lace calico corset round them.*"

6. '*Percy went to Somerton after half sack of trait*' (see diary). In the 1930s farmers would go to Somerton Erleigh Watermill, Lower Somerton, to collect trait (wheatgerm and bran), a byproduct of milling flour, highly valued for finishing off animals before sale or slaughter.

7. The pitch pole on the right was designed to make a tall hayrick before balers were used. A large grab was activated and closed when the weight of the hay was taken by a horse walking forward pulling a rope attached to the grab. Once it was the height of the rick, the pole arm was swung over the rick and the horse made to walk backwards, the grab and load coming to rest on the rick. As the weight was taken off the horse, the grab was hit to release its load. The process was repeated until the rick was built. The stack on the left is last year's hay and has been cut with a hay knife.

8. With the early combine harvesters, a man stood on the side where the wheat came out of a chute in sacks. They were tied up with an ear at each corner, then they were slid down a chute into the field for collection later. The bags were hired from the West of England Sack Contracting Ltd. If you lost one you had to pay ten shillings (50p). Cereals were commonly bought, sold and stored in large jute sacks which held 4 bushels. The bushel was a dry volume measure equivalent to 8 gallons and widely used before the advent of bulk handling of cereal grain in the late 1950s. A sack of wheat weighed 250lbs and farm workers were expected to handle these sacks unassisted, often up steps into grain lofts. In the late 1950s early 1960s with the introduction of health and safety regulations, it became illegal for these sacks to weigh over one hundredweight (112lbs).

9. Thrashing/threshing: in Somerset the word is usually pronounced and written 'thrashing', although the more modern 'threshing' is also used.

10. Lena Kingston, born 1906. The extract is taken from her autobiography 'The Good Old Times' where she describes growing up within a large family and her subsequent life as a cheesemaker. (Somerset Heritage Service Ref: A\DMZ/1/13).

11. The hounds also served a useful purpose within the parish, they were fed on deadstock or slaughtered animals that were too old for use.

WATER AND ELECTRICITY

1. Before the arrival of electricity most wells in the parish were fitted with a hand pump. The village pump stood beside The Old School House, High Ham. The well-head was cemented over when water supplies came to the village. (see photo page 103).

2. Arthur Robinson and his sister travelled by train from Leeds to visit their grandfather, Rev EBA Hughes at the Rectory a number of times before 1939, and were evacuated there for the first nine months of the war.

Professor H. Hale Bellot
1890-1969

3. The photographs of well-heads and water pumps are from '1969 Past in the Present', compiled by Mrs Williams. (Farming footnote 4)
4. The privy at Stembridge Mill (Somerset Heritage Service Ref: A\CLV/1740). Professor Bellot bequeathed Stembridge Windmill to the National Trust 1969.

TRADES AND OTHER WORK

1. Strapper: "*An extra hand, one employed temporarily at harvest time or for thrashing.*" From The West Somerset Word Book by Frederic Thomas Elworthy, pub. 1888. A strapper was also "*someone who took his chance and worked wherever he could*" (Tom Yandle, Exmoor Oral History Archive).
2. Rope: "*The common measure used in husbandry for draining or hedging, also in walling.*" From The West Somerset Word Book by Frederic Thomas Elworthy, pub. 1888
3. Documents have come to light relating to the first wagon ordered in 1912 by WJ Cullen for export to New Zealand. This is a transcript of the letter to FW Lavis dated 30 April 1912 from WJ Cullen, Coombe:

New Years Eve, Kings Head, 1956
Left to right: Andrew Ford, Percy Windsor, L. Hyet, Albert Cullen, G. Tunbridge

"Dear Sir, I herewith enclose a cheque for £20 as promised. I will trust you to make as I say a little wagon as you can and to make the tread of the tire as wide as you can and to make the harvest loader in such a way as to carry the most sacks without spoiling your type or inconveniencing the horse in going over sharp dips. I want you to get it made early as you can so that if I am not quite ready to send it away it can wait a little if it won't inconvenience you. MAHAKIPAWA will be the lettering. Possibly your lettering will be done this way."
There is a Cullensville Road in the Mahakipawa Arm area. It is an agricultural region now part of the Marlborough Wine Region, NZ.
4. There was a stone cutter and quarryman resident in the parish in 1861, possibly working the outcrop of limestone on the slopes above Low Ham. By 1872 a mine for 'plaster stone' had been opened by Barham Brothers of Bridgwater, and in 1881 five stone cutters were living in the parish. (See page 109, photograph of stone crackers).
5. In the parish in 1861 nearly 80 were employed in gloving, mainly women and girls working at home. By 1965 eight were engaged in gloving. There was a glove factory in Langport as early as 1919, and from 1932 a well-known gloving business, Thomas Ensor of Milborne Port, started a factory in Ensor House in Bow Street. In later years it was run by Southcombe and Co and finally Dents who closed in 1971 ending Langport's connection with the gloving industry. (From A History of the County of Somerset, Vol. 8: The Poldens and the Levels, Ed. Robert Dunning, pub. 2004)
6. Extract from Article MT086 Musical Traditions No 2, (see High Days and Holidays footnote 6)
7. In 1851, James Kelway started his nursery business on two acres of land on Picts Hill. By the start of the 20th century it had grown to over 200 acres. He established a world-wide reputation for vegetables and flowers, in particular peonies and irises. Kelways was once one of the largest employers in the area. Information from www.kelways.co.uk
8. The former Rectory, built in 1863, was designed by architect John Norton who had many patrons of wealth and distinction. The Rectory was sold in 1977 (2, Mill Road was purchased for a vicarage in 1983). The rectory was then occupied as a boarding house for Millfield School, Street 1960 to 1977, and from 1978 until the late 1980s was Tor International School, its first pupils coming from South America.

PROVISIONS, PUB, POLICEMAN AND NURSE

1. From the 1965 WI Jubilee Scrapbook recording life in High Ham, Low Ham, Henley and Beer. (Somerset Heritage Service Ref: DD\WI/221/10/2).
2. After High Ham lost its police station, policemen were based at Langport, and included Police Constables: Pitman, Standen, Waites, Davis, Pearce, Lavis, Sparks.

TRANSPORT

1. Brian Howell, a local resident says, "*No clue as to the make of the bike but it's obviously new and she did not stint on the extras – pump, bell and leather tool bag. The front (and only) light is acetylene gas powered and these gave a surprisingly bright light. The thing that dates it is the fact that it has a Sturmey Archer gear system fitted to the rear wheel. If you blow up the photo it has a particular design of gear lever on the handlebar that was only used from 1907. When fitted with the Sturmey Archer gears, the bicycle would have cost around £15. Average wages for manual workers in 1910 were £70 for men and £30 for women per year so this was an expensive machine.*"
2. The Fouracre family also did house clearances, advertising 'Best prices given for antiques and curios'. The shop, in business by 1921, was left to Alfred Stanley Hedgecoe on William's death. Later, it was sold out of the family, and since the 1970s has been a vacant shop still bearing the name Hedgecoe. William (born 1877) and his sons were born in Roman Way in the house next to the shop. William's father (Edwin Henry Fouracre) is the fiddler on page 35.
3. Langport West Station, opened in 1853, was originally called Langport Station until Langport East opened. Langport West was on the Yeovil Branch line, linking to the Bristol to Exeter line at Durston, near Taunton. The station was at Westover. Langport East opened in 1906, on the Castle Cary to Taunton section of the Great Western Railway line. "In the early part of the century visitors from London used this line to visit the splendid sight of peonies at Kelways Nurseries." (Information from The Langport & District History Society website). The stations closed after 1962 as part of the Beeching closures.

118

The Photographs and Memories

The photographs have been loaned to the Parish Community Project by their owners. The quotations are extracts from conversations and interviews made between 2011 and 2014 by members of the High Ham Community Project team. Hard copies and digital files of all material is stored in the village. Also, digital files and hard copies of most photographs and interview transcripts are archived at the Somerset Heritage Centre (see below).

Making a corn mow, Low Ham, 1920s

Turn Hill, 1958. Left to right: Cliff Crossman, Tony Hodge, Mick Sherrin, Ron Wheadon, Jeff Hollard, Ivor Bartlett, Pete Rossiter and Len Cox (seated)

The High Ham Parish Community Project

The High Ham Parish Community Project began with a modest exhibition of old village photographs and memorabilia in 2011. A larger exhibition followed in 2012, the Queen's Silver Jubilee year. Research continued and the archive now contains many hundreds of photographs scanned from residents' family albums, interviews and documents.
The High Ham Parish Community Project is run by five volunteers, all High Ham residents: Amanda Chuter, Caroline Dickens, Sara Ellis, Viv Hall and Kate Lynch. The group focuses on local history and related community projects. It reprinted facsimile copies of the 1965 Women's Institute Scrapbook which was found in the archives at the Somerset Heritage Centre. This led to the High Ham Parish Jubilee Community Scrapbook Project in 2012, when more than 40 residents compiled two volumes documenting life in the villages throughout that year (the original bound volumes are archived at the Somerset Heritage Centre). This is the High Ham Parish Community Project's first published book. It is hoped sales of the book will cover the printing cost and if there is a profit it will be put towards the group's future archive work, exhibitions and events. The High Ham Parish Community Project welcomes further information, photographs, personal family stories and anecdotes, and can be contacted via the website: www.communityhistory.btck.co.uk.

The Somerset Heritage Centre

The Somerset Heritage Centre houses Somerset's archives, local studies library, Historic Environment Record and museum reserve collections, as well as the Somerset Archaeological and Natural History Society library and office. It is the home of the Archives and Local Studies Service, the Heritage Learning team, the Historic Environment Service, the Museums Service and the Victoria County History of Somerset. It is open to the public by appointment.
Somerset Heritage Centre, Langford Mead, Norton Fitzwarren, Taunton, TA2 6SF Tel: 01823 278 805 www.somerset.gov.uk/archives

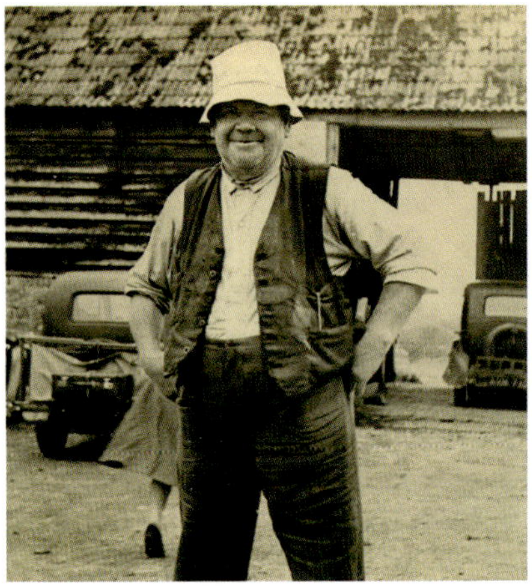